Hope *Faith* Truth

Encouragement for the soul

Dawn Pryor

Ark House Press
PO Box 1722, Port Orchard, WA 98366 USA
PO Box 1321, Mona Vale NSW 1660 Australia
PO Box 318 334, West Harbour, Auckland 0661 New Zealand
arkhousepress.com

© Dawn Pryor 2021

Unless otherwise stated, all Scriptures are taken from the New Living Translation (Holy Bible. New Living Translation copyright© 1996, 2004, 2007, 2013 by Tyndale House Foundation. Used by permission of Tyndale House Publishers Inc., Carol Stream, Illinois 60188. All rights reserved.)

Some names and identifying details have been changed to protect the privacy of individuals.

Cataloguing in Publication Data:
Title: Hope Faith Truth
ISBN: 978-0-6452277-0-3 (pbk)
Subjects: Christian Living;
Other Authors/Contributors: Pryor, Dawn

Cover image courtesy of Sally Kirsch Images
Design by initiateagency.com

May the words on these pages renew your hope, restore your faith, and lead you into a greater truth of Jesus. May you be encouraged, blessed, and inspired.

Love Dawn

God Planned You

Genesis 1:27 (NIV)
'God created mankind in His own image, in the image of God He created them; male and female He created them'

Each and every one of us is a beautiful and perfect creation made by God. We were not an accident, or a mistake, or a surprise, but we were chosen, carefully selected, and made in the image of God.

No matter what you've heard regarding the circumstances of your birth, whether it's been mentioned that your parents never planned you, or that your arrival was an inconvenience, don't for one moment think that you weren't planned by God. Before the beginning of time, He already knew your name, He knew everything about you, and He deeply loved you.

There is no point in time where God looks down on us and thinks to Himself "This one is a mistake, I should never have created her", He would never think that. When God looks at us He is overwhelmed by love, and along with that He is full of pride, and unspeakable joy. We bring Him wonder, and we are a constant source of delight to Him.

Even on our worst days, even when we go against His teachings, when we wander far from Him and make plans that break His heart, it doesn't change His feelings about us. We have been beautifully and fearfully made; we were created in His own image.

When a new mother holds her baby for the first time, she is overwhelmed with love for that child, she has hopes and dreams for them, she would give up her own life for the sake of her little one. This is how God looks at us, in fact He loves us with such a great love, that He sacrificed His own son in order to save us.

Dear friend, whatever you may think of yourself, know that to God you are the world, you are the sun and the moon, you are His own perfect creation, and He will always love you.

Before I was a whisper
Or a thought in the mind
You called me into being
And my destiny you designed.

You prepared for me a purpose
And a path that I would take
You planned for me a future
and the life that I would make.

No matter where I travel
Or how far from you I go
Still you surround me
And it's your presence that I know.

On days when I fail you
Your love still holds me close
You cover me with graciousness
When that's what I need the most.

Lord with all I am I thank you
For the life you breathed in me
For I know that I am chosen
And by your spirit I am free.

Courageous

Psalm 3:3-4 (NCV)
'But Lord, you are my shield, you are my wonderful God who gives me courage. I will pray to the Lord and He will answer me from His mountain'

Our God not only shields us and protects us, but He gives us courage. Courage to stand when our world is crumbling, courage to fight when we feel like giving up, and courage to trust in Him, even when all hope looks lost.

We are so fortunate to have the Spirit of God living in us, and it's His spirit that keeps us going when there seems to be no way forward. It is His Spirit that helps us to live righteous and faithful lives, it's the Holy Spirit of God that intercedes on our behalf, when we are incapable of doing anything for ourselves.

For each of us, in the natural, we face hardships that leave us floundering, we find ourselves overwhelmed by so much that is out of our control, and we walk with fear through situations that come upon us.

But through all of this, we have Jesus. We have the one true God, the one who goes before us, walks beside us, and totally surrounds us, no matter the circumstance. He promises that if we pray, He WILL answer. It's not a maybe, or a possibility, or on the off chance that He's not too busy, but we know, that He will hear us and answer our call.

The bible instructs us to be strong and courageous, and this would be my prayer for each of us, that we would allow our weakness to be overshadowed by God's strength, and that our fears would be diminished, allowing God to pour out on us His courage.

My friends, walk in the courage of God today, no matter what you are facing, and know that when you call on Him, He hears you, He will answer you, and He will shield you through each and every situation you may face.

Lord help me trust in your leading
And walk only in your ways
Leaning not on my own understanding
But knowing you walk with me each day.

Give me courage to face tomorrow
When my soul is drenched in fear
Let me hope in your provision
And believe that you are near.

May I cling to you as my anchor
Knowing I am safe in the storm
That even through life's billows
Around me a shelter you have formed.

I pray for faith that stands steady
Holding on to all that is true
That I would remain faithful
And always find my mind fixed on you.

Thank you Lord for being my fortress
The one I cling to during distress
You fill me with hope and courage
And in you I am blessed.

A Breath of Fresh Air

Job 33:4 (NIV)

'The Spirit of God has made me; the breath of the Almighty gives me life'

We have often heard people or situations described as 'a breath of fresh air'. This can be a much-needed change of attitude, or even scenery. It can be something that's out of the ordinary, or a welcome relief to a situation that is difficult. It can be a beautiful soul speaking blessing over us, or it can be the wind blowing through a dry and barren place, changing the atmosphere, and making things bearable again. It can be the falling rain after a relentless dry hot summer, or it can be the beginning of spring, with new life all around us after the cold, wet, winter.

A breath of fresh air is what God is to us, He is our refreshment, the one who gives us life. He takes what was lost, what we thought had died and He breathes into it, restoring it to fullness again.

When God made us, He made us for greatness, for hope and for purpose. However, sometimes we lose our way, we stray off the path He has for us, and we end up in places we were never meant to be. We decide on a path and go about making choices of our own, and sometimes these choices can impact our lives in ways we would never have expected. Yet God never leaves us. He continues to walk with us, on our good days and our bad days, and through it all He continues to fill our lungs with His breath, as He gently whispers His love over us.

Be encouraged today that the same God whose very breath created the universe, made you, and He is continuing to breathe new life into you, He is bringing resurrection into your barren places, and walking you into His hope, His plan, and His purpose for your life.

This is the goodness of our Almighty God.

I stand in awe of your creation
Of all that you have done
You breathed life into perfection
You made the stars, the moon, the sun.

All of nature is your masterpiece
Made and formed by you
Beautifully put together
Coloured in perfect hues.

On the days before you rested
You planted deep into the ground
All for our enjoyment
Such beauty can be found.

Palms that sway in breezes
Giving shelter from the heat
With amazing fronds abounding
We are truly blessed indeed.

So God I thank you for these pleasures
All your hands have made and more
I give you all the glory
As I'm forever grateful Lord.

Trust in Him

2 Timothy 1:7 (NKJV)
'For God has not given us a spirit of fear, but of power, love and a sound mind'

We all know that fear, worry, concern or anxiety does not come from God. Yet in times of crisis, or in hard situations, our mind tends to go into these thought patterns.

We buy into the lie that we should be fearful or anxious, that we should worry, or be filled with doubt, because we don't know what the future will look like. Yet we do know what God looks like, we know His nature and we know that in all things He is in control.

God gives us strength, which is another word for power. We have strength to face each day and all that it brings. He gives us love, and we know that love, His perfect love, casts out all fear. And He gives us a sound mind, a mind that knows without a shadow of a doubt, that our God goes before us in all things, and He is with us through all things.

So therefore, knowing that we have all these things from God, we can make a conscious decision to put aside all that which would cause us to be anxious, to lay it at His feet, and to move into a place of trust in Him.

So, for today, and throughout this week, put aside all your concerns, your worries and your anxieties, and know that our God, the almighty God, already has everything in hand, and He has a plan for each one of us regardless of how bad the situation might look.

He is for us in all things, He surrounds us, and He goes before us, therefore we have nothing to fear.

Let's continue to put our trust in Him, and to know that He has everything in hand.

Your promise is for perfect peace
For those who trust in you
So I lay down all my burdens
And I wait patiently on your truth.

I know your eye is on the sparrow
And you see what lies ahead
You will always be beside me
And by your spirit I am led.

I hope only in your goodness
As I go forth from day to day
You cover me with protection
As I walk in all your ways.

I thank you for your guidance
And that I live without fear
My mind Lord I keep on you
And sense your presence here.

Body, soul, and spirit
I submit all I am to you
For you're the Alpha and Omega
You are the God of all truth.

God Has A Plan

Jeremiah 29:11 (NIV)

"For I know the plans I have for you," declares the Lord, "plans to prosper you and not to harm you, plans to give you hope and a future"

Each of us go through our lives making plans. From choosing a path that we want to travel, making career choices, finding a partner, and forging our way in the world. We are constantly making some sort of plan or decision that will direct our future towards an outcome of our choosing. We are always hopeful that our plans will benefit us, that they will give us purpose, and that they will provide us with deep satisfaction.

When our plans go astray, we feel lost, or we become unhinged. We may not have a backup plan, and we worry about the next step, what we will do, and where we will go.

Yet God tells us that HE has a plan for us, a plan that includes hope and a future. His plan is not built on choices we've made, but on His promises to us.

His promise includes prospering us and not causing us harm. It's about providing us with a future that is built on His hope. It's about leading us in a direction that will be beneficial for us and bring about fruitfulness in our lives.

If today your life doesn't look the way you thought it would, or your plans aren't playing out in the way your dreams projected they would, don't feel despondent and don't give up. God knew before the beginning of time exactly what path you would be on, where you would be today and where you are heading tomorrow. He still has a plan, a good plan for your life.

Continue to invite God into every decision that you make and know that He will be with you every step of the way on your journey.

Let us remember to 'acknowledge Him in all our ways, and He will direct our paths' (Proverbs 3:6).

Lord I bring my prayers before you
And ask that you would search my heart
Lead me by your spirit
And from me don't depart.

Let me know where you are calling
And where you would have me to go
So that I might be a blessing
To all those that I know.

Show me your plan and purpose
For how to live my life
That I might be your servant
And into darkness bring your light.

Hear the words that I am whispering
And my cries called out to you
Listen to my voice of hope
As I walk upright in your truth.

For I will follow where you lead me
And be guided by your hand
Step by step into the future
Into the life that you have planned.

Waiting on God

Micah 7:7 (NCV)

'I will look to the Lord for help. I will wait for God to save me. My God will hear me'

We all know what it's like to be in a state of waiting. During this season of Covid-19 we've all felt like a plane on the runway, in a state of holding, not quite knowing when our turn to move forward will come. We feel like we're in exile, forgotten and left alone with no hope for the future.

For those of us who have lived through a number of lockdowns, it has left us feeling isolated and alone. The days stretch into weeks, and then months, with no hope of any change, and with very little to look forward to. Every day is the same, we just wait for the news to come that this time is over, and life can start again.

Yet this is our perfect opportunity, that while we are waiting in the natural, we also need to be waiting in the spiritual. We need to be waiting on God, knowing that He is our help, that if we look for Him, and call out to Him, then He will hear us.

It would never be God's intention for us to feel abandoned or exiled, but it is during these times that God wants us to wait on Him, to hear what He has to say, to seek Him in all that we do. He promises that He will hear us, but He can't hear if we don't call out, we need to take an active part in order to receive the blessing of His promise.

Today let's aim to turn our focus off the negative of waiting, and onto the positive, having great expectation for all the Lord is going to do. Let's see this time as a moment of preparation for a future of blessing.

Take time out this week to wait on God, to hear what He has to say, and allow Him to renew us, to change us from the inside out, and become who He is calling us to be.

As I stand waiting in the hallway
For you to open up the door
I will praise you for your goodness
And give thanks that I am yours.

I will hold onto your promises
And trust you with my heart
As I walk forward to new beginnings
And the hope of a new start.

For I trust in your timing
Although it's not like mine
And though the waiting seems eternal
I give my life to the divine.

So as doors close all around me
I keep my eyes placed on you
And I live in expectation
That my God will bring me through.

For it's in the hallway I learn patience
And my faith is stretched once more
For it's here I'm in your presence
As I lay my life before you Lord.

Contentment in God

1 Timothy 6:6-8 (NIV)
'But godliness with contentment is great gain. For we brought nothing into the world, and we can take nothing out of it. But if we have food and clothing, we will be content with that'

Contentment is one of those areas in life that we all need to learn at a much greater level. For many of us, feeling settled with what we have and where we are is more difficult than it really should be. We live in a world where all that we want can be achieved relatively easily, so there is no need to remain in our current situation, or with what we already have, as moving forward is quite attainable.

However, there are times when our plans don't go as we thought they would, our financial situation changes, and our dreams get put on hold. That's when we need to move our focus off all that seems lost or out of reach and learn to be still and content with each new day.

Sometimes when we look at our current situation it can be easy to be miserable and discontent, yet we know that our greatest satisfaction can never be met by earthly things, it can only be found in the long-lasting spiritual joy and strength of the Lord.

When our days on earth have come to an end, we will leave exactly the same way we arrived, with nothing. It seems we spend all our working days accumulating 'stuff', however when we breathe our last breath, everything is left behind and we go to meet our Maker with only our spirit, and nothing more.

Today let us all lift our eyes off our circumstances, what we may or may not have, and place them on God. Let us find contentment regardless of what we're walking through and let us trust Him to be the true source of love, joy, health, peace and strength in our lives.

Lord teach me to be grateful
Even when there's nothing good I see
Remind me of your faithfulness
And your everlasting love for me.

Help me to find the value
of the beauty in each day
To look for the silver lining
And reflect on this as I pray.

Show me the miracle of creation
And let me be in awe
By all your hand has fashioned
That is right outside my door.

Let me rise up in thankfulness
Giving all glory unto you
For even on the hardest days
I know your Word is truth.

So may my spirit be attuned to you
As I choose to bring you praise
And as you teach me to be grateful
I bless you Lord this day.

Good News

Luke 4:18 (NIV)

'The Spirit of the Lord is on me, because He has anointed me to proclaim good news to the poor. He has sent me to proclaim freedom for the prisoners and recovery of sight for the blind, to set the oppressed free'

Each one of us has the spirit of the Lord on us, we have all been anointed by God. This isn't something special that is only for pastors, evangelists or missionaries, this is for each of us. God has called us all to 'Go into all the world and preach the gospel' (Mark 16:15), this includes you and me. He wants us to take the promise of eternal life to those who need to hear it.

The ability to proclaim good news is within us, and there is nothing more that is needed in the world right now than good news. Our world has turned into a place filled with hate and violence, of hopelessness and fear. We are surrounded by friends and family, colleagues and neighbours who are lost and who are suffering, right now they need to hear the good news of Christ.

Because of Jesus, we can proclaim freedom, we can share about His mercy and grace, we can bring hope into dark and broken situations. We have His heart within us, that we might go out and love those who feel unloved, and care for those who can no longer care for themselves.

We are living amongst those who are oppressed, who are living under a cloud of heaviness, living in doubt and fear, and it is up to us, to you and to me, those whom the spirit of the Lord is upon, to bring them good news, to show them the way to freedom and to lead them into the truth of Jesus.

I encourage you this week to find the lost, the lonely, and the hurt, and to proclaim the good news to those who need to hear it.

In a world that's filled with darkness
Where hope cannot be found
I will cry out the name of Jesus
As my love for Him abounds.

There is no other God besides Him
He is the beginning and the end
The Alpha and Omega
The one I call true friend.

He is the good news to the hurting
To the broken and the lost
For them He bore the sacrifice
With His death on the cross.

He is the answer to our questions
The hope for all mankind
The miracle of salvation
He brings healing to the mind.

Let the goodness of Christ Jesus
Be the balm to your soul
That in His truth you find redemption
And in His love be made whole.

Guard Your Mind

2 Corinthians 10:5 (NIV)
'We demolish arguments and every pretension that sets itself up against the knowledge of God, and we take captive every thought to make it obedient to Christ'

The words 'what if' can lead us into a downward spiral, where we allow our imagination to take us into dark places that we were never intended to go.

The Bible tells us to keep our minds fixed on Christ, and in doing this we are focusing on what is good and what is true. It's in the moments when we take our eyes and our minds off Jesus that we find ourselves in trouble.

It's easy to walk in negativity, to explore the darker side of life. We can go so quickly from feeling good about ourselves and our situation to suddenly becoming overwhelmed and weighed down by the thoughts that seemingly attack us from out of nowhere.

We know that the mind is a dangerous and powerful battleground. It's where the devil will fight his hardest to entice us into believing toxic thoughts. If we allow him to win this battle, then he has an open door into all areas of our lives.

Guard your mind with all you have, watch over your thoughts and be quick to reign in anything that pulls you away from what you know to be the truth. We need to daily put on the full armour of God, so that we are prepared in all situations, and that we are covered by the full protection that we need to fight the good fight.

God wants us to live our lives free from the darkness that surrounds us, to think on whatever is pure and lovely, and don't let the devil have a foothold over you. 'So therefore, fix your mind on things above and walk steadfastly in the promises of God' (Colossians 3:2).

I would encourage you today to think about what you're thinking about and ask Jesus to fill your mind with only that which is good, and that is from Him.

In the midst of all my chaos
When my mind will not relent
When the darkness tries to own me
And my heart is bruised and bent.

It's there in the silence
That your still small voice is clear
You whisper to me gently
And calm me of my fears.

Your words bring peace and healing
As you gently speak my name
And I feel you breathe upon me
As my spirit lifts again.

Your breath of life fulfils me
As the balm to my soul
And a weight lifts off my shoulders
As I feel myself let go.

For I hear your voice remind me
As it tells me to be still
And with your blessed reassurance
I commit my way unto your will.

He is With Us Always

Jeremiah 33:3 (GNT)

'Call to me and I will answer you. I will tell you wonderful and marvelous things you could never figure out on your own'

This scripture is such a beautiful gift to be given to us. The promise that when we call to God, He will answer us.

So often in life we are let down and disappointed by people. We think we can rely on others, yet they are nowhere to be seen when we need them.

It will never be like this with God, He is always available for us, always willing to hear our call. There is never a time that God would turn His back on us or be too busy when we need Him.

When we read further on in this verse it goes on to say that God will tell us wonderful things that we could never figure out on our own.

In our lives there are just so many things we struggle to figure out, things that worry us, cause us confusion or anxiety, or things that we just don't understand. Yet, God in His amazing love for us, answers our call and helps us sort through all the difficulties that we are faced with.

If you think that no one is on your side, or has your back, you can think again, because God certainly does. When we feel lost, God is guiding us. When we feel alone, God has us surrounded. When we are fearful, God offers us His peace. When we are worn out, God carries us. When we are empty, God fills us with His spirit.

There is no situation that God is not with us, providing for us, leading us, and strengthening us.

If we allow Him, God will be our ever-present help in times of need. He is the God of today, tomorrow and forever.

There is nothing that is too hard for Him, and nothing He wouldn't do for us, so call on Him today, knowing that in all things, and through all things, He will be with you.

I hear your voice when all is silent
Speaking gently over me
Whispering words in the darkness
Offering love, hope, and peace.

When my soul is low and downcast
And my mind controls my ways
Your breath of life restores me
And upholds me through the day.

I rely upon your presence
And place my life into your hands
Guide me Lord in all I do
And show me of your plans.

For when I'm weak you are my tower
And when I'm down you are my rock
My fortress in the valley
My strength, my life, my God.

Be my everlasting peace I pray
Breathe life into my soul
For without you I am nothing
But by your Spirit I am whole.

Just Believe

Mark 5:36 (NIV)

Jesus said to Him "Don't be afraid, just believe"

There are so many times in our lives when we want to believe, we desperately need to believe, yet we are overcome by doubt and fear.

In this Bible passage a father has asked Jesus to come to his house to heal his daughter, but as they arrive, he's told that his daughter has already died, so he should stop bothering Jesus.

What a terrible situation. If we were to put ourselves into this man's shoes, we would be totally overcome. We would be overwhelmed by feelings of despair, hopelessness, grief, hurt and bewilderment. However, Jesus tells him not to be afraid or fearful, not to listen to the voices around him, but to just believe and trust.

How often do we find ourselves walking through situations in our lives where we are overwhelmed, knocked down, fearful and defeated? We are listening to all those around us who are giving us negative and unhelpful advice, we are filled with hurt and unspeakable pain, and there appears to be no end to our disappointment and heartbreak.

The answer Jesus gives us is the same as what He gave this father, He wants us to close our ears to the voices around us, let go of all the fear that we are facing, and trust wholeheartedly in Him. He wants us to stop opening up our lives to lies and deception, and to place our hope and our faith in Him.

Be encouraged today that the same Jesus who can raise the dead to life, can most certainly walk with you through any hardships you may be facing. All He asks is that you block out the noise that surrounds you, bring your focus onto Him, and believe that He can do abundantly more than you hoped or dreamed.

He is the God of miracles and change, hold on to this truth today, and let Him walk with you through your fear, and out the other side.

By the power of His spirit
May you live by faith alone
May the warrior inside you
Rise up to the unknown.

May you be surrounded by His presence
And led daily by His grace
As you live your life courageously
And soak in His embrace.

Fear not for He is with you
And goes before you in all ways
His strength will be your portion
As you face the start of each new day.

So live your life victoriously
Be filled with hope renewed
Trust alone in His promises
As you hold onto His truth.

Let His spirit rise within you
As you walk daily in His plan
May His power be your portion
And by His strength may you stand.

Rest in Him

Mark 6:31 (NLT)

Jesus said "Let's go off by ourselves to a quiet place and rest awhile"

What a refreshing thing it is to know that even Jesus got tired, and that He and His disciples took time out to rest. He recognised that in the busyness of all that was going on around Him, the constant coming and going, the demands on His time, it was important to just stop.

We live in a world that is consumed with 'doing', where we always need to have something on the go at all times, and it can appear selfish or lazy to just want to jump off the merry-go-round and take some time out for ourselves.

This is especially prevalent amongst young mothers, they can find themselves in a constant state of exhaustion, the demands on their time never seem to let up as they face the ongoing workload of babies and children. Unfortunately, society has made them feel guilty if they so much as voice that they would like to just stop, take some time out for themselves, and get away.

However, we read in this verse that Jesus fully advocates the need for rest, He tells His disciples that they need to get away, to take a break. There is no guilt being laid on them for not pushing on, but they are encouraged to just take some time out.

Jesus was just like us in the physical, He needed refreshment, He needed solitude, He needed time to be restored.

We too need this, we need at times to draw away from others, take some time for ourselves, to recharge our batteries, refill our tanks, tune into God, and then continue on our journey.

If you find today that you're running on empty, you're weary and you've got nothing left to give, just stop. Take the time out you need, without feeling guilty, and just rest, knowing that if Jesus took time to recharge, then its ok for you to do it too.

Rest in Him.

When I wait in your presence
And sit quietly in your peace
I feel my soul rest in silence
As my mind finds release.

I let go of all my burdens
As I give myself to you
I offer up all I am
And you wash over me with truth.

I relinquish all that I control
And lay it at your feet
For I know it's in the letting go
Where you and I will meet.

I raise my hands in surrender
And bow my heart unto yours
I worship you in spirit
And meditate daily on your laws.

Here I am Lord for your glory
Take my life and make it shine
With the love and grace of Jesus
As to Him I am entwined.

His Hands and Feet

Luke 10:33-34 (NCV)

'Then a Samaritan travelling down the road came to where the hurt man was lying. He saw the man and felt very sorry for him. The Samaritan went to him and poured oil and wine on his wounds and bandaged them. He put the hurt man on his donkey and took him to the inn. At the inn the Samaritan took care of him'

This scripture is our blueprint for life, to be the hands and feet of Jesus in caring for others. We are called to go the extra mile, to give from our abundance, so that all those around us would see Jesus through us.

Before the Samaritan came across this man, two others had passed him by, neither of them took the time to help the man in need, they chose instead to cross to the other side of the road. These weren't bad men, they just weren't willing to get involved, so they turned a blind eye, and in doing so they missed their opportunity to show the love of God to someone in need.

Each of us, in some way, is surrounded by those in need, if not physically, then most definitely mentally and spiritually. We all have family, friends and neighbours who God has called us to care for.

There are wounded people all around us, people who need to know they are loved, who need cared for, who need a touch of healing that goes deeper than anything doctors, and medicine can provide.

This week, let's all be that good Samaritan, let's not pass by on the other side, but let's actively love those who God puts on our path, and pray that He would expand our view so that we can see the needs of those around us. Let's be the hands and feet of Jesus in a world of hurt people.

To be the hands and feet of Jesus
Showing compassion, love and care
Going further than expected
When others heavy loads we bear.

Being the shoulder on the hard days
For tears and heavy hearts
Showing up and being the difference
Offering love from the start.

A word of kindness brings refreshment
To a wounded soul in the dark
For when all seems lost and empty
Just one word can light the spark.

To fill the void of hopelessness
To where joy can find a way
Bringing Jesus to the hurting
For this is what we pray.

Lord give us opportunities
That the lost may come to you
That the unravelled find your mercy
And are healed by your truth.

Blessings and Renewal

Joel 2:25 (NIV)

'I will repay you for the years that the locusts have eaten'

What a beautiful promise of hope, that our God, in His loving kindness would repay us for ALL that the locusts have stolen. That no matter what has been devoured, or snatched away from us, God would give back to us – pressed down, shaken together, and running over.

When a plague of locusts' swarm, their numbers are so great that they can spread out across sixty countries. They attack crops, devouring everything in sight, and completely wiping out everything in their path.

For many of us, we have had so many areas of our lives stolen or devoured, this could be our health, our dreams, our family, or the things that we've yearned for. We may have gone through months or years of struggling, of barely holding on or getting by. Everything that we had placed our hopes in, seems to have been taken from us, leaving us feeling depleted and let down.

Maybe you have lost your job or received a bad health report that has knocked the wind out of you, or maybe the marriage you had thought would last has suddenly ended. Everything that you had based your security in is gone, and you're feeling lost and empty.

But we can take hope, and rest in the knowledge, that our God is still with us in the midst of our darkest days, and He will give back all that we have lost.

As you have pushed through, trusted and remained faithful, the almighty God will repay you in abundance, and He will bless and renew you.

The old things are gone, but all that remains and is yet to come will bring new life to you, as you continue to place your hope and faith in Him.

Lord you are my provider
The holder of my cup
You fill my life with goodness
As you continue to hold me up.

When I thought all hope had ended
And all provision had run dry
When I doubted in your kindness
And thought you love for me had died.

It was then I read your promises
That for all that I had lost
You would repay to overflowing
No matter what the cost.

You gave back all that was stolen
And you filled my life anew
That I would know your blessings
And would give glory back to you.

For all the locusts had devoured
You gave, and gave some more
So in gratefulness I praise you
My Lord, my God, my all.

Be at Peace

John 16:33 (NIV)

"I have told you these things, so that in me you may have peace. In this world you will have trouble, but take heart!! I have overcome the world."

We all know how it feels to live without peace, to live our lives full of chaos, and to be in a state of disorganised mess.

Each of us has experienced times in our lives where we don't know what the future will hold, we don't know how we will make it from one day to the next. We have found ourselves worried and anxious over anything and everything, be it our health, finances, family or our career

Each of us desperately needs to feel the peace of God.

Jesus tells us that in this world we will have trouble. It's no surprise to Him, and therefore, it should be no surprise to us. But His promise to us through our trouble, is His peace. Not peace that the world can give, that is short lived and based on circumstances, but peace that passes all understanding, and that can only come from God.

It is a peace that permeates through our body, soul and spirit. It doesn't discount what is going on around us, but it rises above it. This kind of peace brings us back into alignment with how God wants us to live, it replaces our fear with calm, and allows us to know that no matter what happens, we can trust that God is taking care of us.

Today I pray that your life would be built on the peace that comes from Jesus, that you would allow Him to flood your being with rest, with trust, with hope and with joy. May your mind be renewed, and your spirit be filled, as you lean in deeper to the power of God's love, and let His peace be what sustains you today, tomorrow and always.

In the trials and the tempest
When my soul cannot find peace
I cling to my Saviour
And I wait for quiet release.

When hope feels so far away
And darkness fills the sky
I still place my faith in Jesus
And know He holds me tight.

For though my circumstance is shaky
And the ground I walk gives way
My trust is in my redeemer
As I know for me, He makes a way.

So I rest in His assurance
And stand firm in His embrace
For no matter what comes against me
I fight whatever giant I may face.

For it's in the trial and the tempest
Where my strength will be renewed
Where Christ meets me in the battle
And the mountain before me is removed.

Jesus Our Example

---

2 Peter 1:5-7 (NIV)
'For this reason, make every effort to add to your faith goodness, and to goodness, knowledge; and to knowledge, self-control; and to self-control, perseverance; and to perseverance, godliness; and to godliness, mutual affection, love'

This is such a powerful scripture which outlines all of the attributes a christian should endeavour to have. It is not enough to just have a faith, but we need to add to that faith.

To grow in the Lord, we need to take on His characteristics, we should be desiring to be more like Him in all ways. Growth requires discipline, and a deliberate decision to follow or chase after that which we want.

Jesus was the perfect example of how we should live. He was filled with goodness, His entire life was dedicated to service, to caring for and loving others. There is no greater outworking of goodness than this. He was full of knowledge; He understood His purpose and He fulfilled it. Throughout his life, He was never without self-control, He never gave in to temptation, no matter how good and promising it looked. He showed us the way of perseverance, He pushed on regardless of what it would cost Him, even His life. Jesus was God, He was made in the image of God and therefore godliness was the character of who He was. And finally, we know, Jesus is love. No greater love than He who lays His life down for His friends (John 15:13).

Everything that Jesus was we should aim to be, He was the perfect christian, He led others by His example, and in Him there was no fault.

My encouragement for all of us today, is that we would add to our faith, that we would discipline ourselves to grow in Jesus, and in doing so we would take on His characteristics and learn from Him.

May each of us walk, blameless, in the faith we have been called to.

Lord you lead by your example
Of all that we should be
The life we should be living
The hope that sets us free.

We see in you the goodness
And the affection from God above
How you lavish us with kindness
And wash over us with love.

You're the God of perseverance
Who stands strong through it all
You rise up against deception
To fight our foe and his foils.

In you there is knowledge
The answer we all seek
You are faithful to guide us
You're our strength when we are weak.

Lord we thank you for all you teach us
Through your life we are free
We walk with you to eternity
Where your face we will see.

Step Out With Courage

Matthew 14:25-31 (NIV)

'Shortly before dawn Jesus went out to them, walking on the lake. When the disciples saw him walking on the lake, they were terrified. "It's a ghost," they said, and cried out in fear. But Jesus immediately said to them: "Take courage! It is I. Don't be afraid." "Lord, if it's you," Peter replied, "tell me to come to you on the water." "Come," he said. Then Peter got down out of the boat, walked on the water and came toward Jesus. But when he saw the wind, he was afraid and, beginning to sink, cried out, "Lord, save me!" Immediately Jesus reached out His hand and caught him. "You of little faith," He said, "why did you doubt?"

When we read this scripture, we focus on Peter's fear and lack of faith, rather than on the courage Peter had in getting out of the boat.

This story isn't just about a man who took his eyes off Jesus, this is about one man's courage to walk toward Jesus, in the middle of a lake, during the midst of a storm.

There were twelve men in that boat, yet only one of them had the courage to ask Jesus if he could walk on water and come to Him. Only one was willing to get out of the safety of the boat and face the unknown. Even though all twelve men had been with Jesus, and had seen Him perform many miracles, only one was willing to risk everything to move closer to Him.

It takes courage to make a stand, to trust that God will hold you in the hard times, and to focus on the one who is calling you closer to Him.

Peter would have been fearful getting out of the boat, and stepping into the stormy water, but he put aside that fear and courageously took his first steps towards Jesus.

Whatever boat you find yourself in today, whatever storm requires your courage, step into it, and trust that God will hold you. Don't let fear hold you back from what Jesus is calling you into.

As the waves crash around me
And my boat rocks to and fro
I cry out to you in fearfulness
And pray you won't let me go.

I am surrounded on all sides
And my courage is all but gone
I'm trusting in your faithfulness
As I try to stay strong.

I step out in faith to reach you
Looking not left nor right
But keeping my eyes upon you
And trusting you have me in your sight.

Though my heart knows you are with me
The storm within me pulls me down
So Lord I cry out for your mercy
Please don't let me drown.

Walk with me dear Jesus
From the boat onto dry land
And fill my heart with courage
Give me faith that I might stand.

Be Joyful

1 Thessalonians 5:16 (NIV)
'Rejoice Always'

God's will for us is to live our lives filled with joy, that in the midst of any and every circumstance we are able to find our joy in Him, and to give thanks to Him.

There are times in life that we can struggle with this, we have so many things going on in us and around us, that often enough we find it increasingly difficult to remain joyful. Instead, we find ourselves filled with worry, or fear, or hurt, or disappointment, and our season of life has stripped us of all opportunity to feel anything remotely like joy.

In these times, it's important to remember that joy and happiness are not necessarily the same thing. We get our happiness from external things, such as people, places and events, whereas, our joy is internal, and comes from having peace and being settled, regardless of what is happening all around us.

James 1:2 says 'Consider it pure joy my brothers whenever you face trials of many kinds'. James is not suggesting that we be happy during our trials, but he knows that we can have joy, even in our suffering.

Jesus is our source of joy, He is the giver of life, He is the hope of our tomorrow, and He is our anchor in the storm. He is with us always, and in Him we need never be alone. There is great joy to be found in this, that regardless of what we are going through, we have the God of all life, hope and peace walking with us through our difficult circumstances.

Today I would encourage you, in the midst of whatever you're facing, that you would look up and not down. That you would turn your face upon Jesus, and that you would allow Him to reignite the joy within your heart.

Lord fill my heart with joyfulness
For all that comes from you
Let my spirit bubble over
With the power of your truth.

May I see goodness all around me
Even on my darkest days
That I would walk in your faithfulness
And trust you in all my ways.

Give me joy in every circumstance
That I might be at peace
That I can rise above my problems
And trust you in between.

Let me sing songs of goodness
Of your hope and your love
That I would be filled to overflowing
Abundant blessings from above.

So Lord teach me to be joyful
Even when my eyes don't see
But to trust in your promises
And your faithfulness to me.

Living Waters

Isaiah 43:18-19 (NIV)

'Forget the former things; do not dwell in the past. See, I am doing a new thing! Now it springs up, do you not perceive it? I am making a way in the wilderness and streams in the wasteland.'

God calls each of us to look forward and not back.

He doesn't want us to be held back by the past, but He wants us to move forward with all that He has ahead for us.

It can be very difficult when we're walking through our wilderness to not look back at what our lives used to be like. It's hard not to wish things were different during what appears to be a season of waste. Yet, God tells us that He is doing a new thing, something we have never experienced before. He is making a way in the wilderness, so although we feel like we are in a desolate place, He is preparing our path with what we need to move us forward into all that He has for us.

Sometimes we can experience hardship and pain, loneliness and despair, and we can't understand why God would let us go through this, however, in the midst of this, He also surprises us with blessings and moments of joy that we weren't expecting. This is our streams in the wasteland. The Bible describes streams as 'living water', this is what Jesus is to us, He is our living water. In the middle of our darkest days, and our desolate seasons, He provides us with living water for our thirsty souls. His living water encourages growth and change, and it brings resurrection to all that we thought had died.

If your days are filled with continually looking back, try looking up, take the focus off 'what was' and onto 'what will be'.

God's promise to us is that He will do a new thing, all we have to do is trust Him and His timing.

Let's be excited for what He has ahead for us.

My God you are my living water
My hope when all is lost
My streams in the desert
The one who paid the cost.

Your spring wells up inside of me
Bringing life into these bones
You walk with me through the wilderness
And prepare a place that is my home.

You carry me through the dark days
And bring me joy instead of tears
You comfort me in the hard times
And in you I have no fear.

When I turn my eyes toward your promise
And lean in towards your love
You quench this thirsty soul of mine
With refreshment from above.

I declare that I will follow
And trust you all my days
For you've led me from the wasteland
And in you my heart will stay.

A Life of Abundance

John 10.10 (NIV)
'The thief comes only to kill, steal and destroy, I have come that they may have life, and that they may have it more abundantly'

This is such a powerful verse that portrays so well the fight we are in, and the battle we are walking through. This is the truth of Jesus versus the deception of the devil.

Jesus came that our lives would be full and rich, overflowing with goodness. That we would have strength, be filled with peace, be full of joy, and be blessed. This is His plan and His purpose for each of our lives.

However, the devil wants to steal all of that from us, He wants to take all the good and strip it away so that we are left with nothing. He wants us to believe that we don't deserve to live full and vibrant lives, that we can't expect anything good to happen to us, or for us. He wants us to listen to the lies that tell us we're not good enough, we haven't worked hard enough, and we're not loved enough. He wants to take what Jesus did on the cross for us and make it insignificant.

Don't let him!!

Jesus fought for you, and He died for you, He went willingly to the cross, that your life would be of value. He has purpose for you, your life matters, therefore what you do and what you think matters. Jesus came to give us abundant lives, that we would have more than enough of anything we need. Don't let the devil steal all that you have, your health, your family, your finances and most importantly your heart. Know who you are, live a life of purpose, full and overflowing; take back all that the devil has tried to steal, and walk forward in your promise and your purpose, live your life of abundance.

There are lies and deceptions
That come to steal your peace
That will leave you feeling broken
And fill you with disease.

It's the work of the darkness
to infiltrate your soul
to rob you of your faith in Christ
and destroy all that's whole.

But let the truth be your deliverance
As you cling to God alone
That you would know His faithfulness
And in Him would be at home.

Trust in His provisions
As you place your hope in His plan
That you would live a life of abundance
And in Him you would stand.

Let your faith be your hiding place
Your fortress and your tower
Where the truth and love of Jesus
Give your strength, hope and power.

Unforced Rhythm of Grace

Matthew 11:28-30 (MSG)

'Are you tired? Worn out? Burned out on religion? Come to me. Get away with me and you will recover your life. I will show you how to take a real rest. Walk with me and work with me—watch how I do it. Learn the unforced rhythms of grace. I won't lay anything heavy or ill-fitting on you. Keep company with me and you'll learn to live freely and lightly.'

We all know the busyness of life. The frantic pace at which we seem to work, that leaves us worn out and exhausted. There are some days when we are so tired, we can barely put one foot in front of the other. Jesus calls us to get away from this, to walk with Him into a life of rest and recovery.

He knows, and understands full well, from His own life experience, how easy it is to become tired and worn out.

Sometimes we think it is only us, those of us in the 21st century, who know what it's like to be fatigued. Yet, Jesus Himself faced times of being completely wiped out. He had people following Him everywhere He went, making constant demands on His time, and always needing something from Him. He taught the crowds who followed Him, and He fed the masses who were always surrounding Him, so He knew what it was to be burned out.

During these times, He went off by Himself, and found His refreshment in God. He spent His time praying and interceding, and this is where He found and regained His strength.

Jesus is calling us to do the same thing today. He wants us to get away with Him and rest. He promises He won't lay anything heavy on us, but that if keep company with Him, we will learn to live freely and lightly.

Today if you're feeling overwhelmed and exhausted, get away with Jesus and let Him refresh your soul, and teach you His unforced rhythms of grace.

When my body feels depleted
And my soul has no rest
I cling to my redeemer
And trust that He knows best.

When the world is filled with chaos
And hope feels lost at sea
I know who holds my future
For the breath of life is holding me.

In all my days of busyness
When my feet don't touch the ground
I hold on to my saviour
For that's where my hope is found.

When I feel life is overwhelming
And there seems no end in sight
I spend time in God's presence
For it's He who makes things right.

In everything, there is Jesus
He is my beginning and my end
I choose to trust in His promises
My Lord, my God, my friend.

Our Safe House

Psalm 9:9-10 (MSG)

'God is a safe house for the battered, a sanctuary during bad times. The moment you arrive, you relax, you're never sorry that you knocked'

This promise is such an amazing revelation, and the most wonderful gift to hold onto.

God is a safe house for the battered. I am sure that there have been times in all of our lives when we have felt battered, when our relationships haven't worked out like we thought they would, when finances have caused us to lose what we held dear, or when all that we had placed our security in was suddenly taken from us, leaving us terrified of what the future would hold. There are times when we walk through a season of illness that we become overwhelmed, whether it is our own illness or a family member, it can feel like we have been completely side-swiped, and it drains us of all hope and peace.

At times like this, God becomes our sanctuary, He becomes our anchor, the place where we can go with all our despair, our tears, and our anxiety. He is our hiding place, the hope that we cling to, and the rock that we hide under. There is nothing better than knowing that we have a haven in our storm, a shelter that protects us during our hardest season, and a place where we can let go of everything that has left us bruised and battered.

It is such a comfort to us to know that we can take our wounded spirit, and our fragile emotions to God, our sanctuary, and in Him we will find our rest.

Let this be the hope that you hold on to, that you can take refuge in our God, know that He is your safe-house, and the one you can place your hope in during your time of need.

When clouds hide my vision
And my eyes can't see ahead
I press in and trust you deeper
Believing in all you've said.

When I doubt my own decisions
And know I need to turn to you
I lay my burdens at your footstool
And cling with might to your truth.

For in the passion of your purpose
My heart remains the same
That I will follow in your calling
And be transfixed by your gaze.

Walk with me through indecision
May your voice be all I hear
That I would tune in to your spirit
And your peace would drown out my fear.

Let me trust you in the darkness
As I walk forward in my faith
That you would be my hiding place
The home where I am safe.

Don't Live in Disappointment

Psalm 119:116 (NIV)

'Sustain me, my God, according to your promise, and I will live, do not let my hopes be dashed'

We all face many seasons in our life, and some of them are harder than others. One of these seasons is disappointment, where our soul feels crushed, and we're not sure how we can move forward.

Having moments of disappointment is not the problem, it's when we choose to live in our disappointment, rather than moving on. The bigger picture is realising that this isn't the end of our story, God never leaves us in our heartache, but He leads us to better things.

If the door is closed, if the hurt is still there, if the diagnosis looks bleak, just keep going. God has better days ahead, if only we can hold on.

God's word has promises of hope, of joy, of abundance, of living a full life. One set back is not the final chapter. Tears and despair don't mean the end of the world, it just means we need to hold on even tighter to Jesus and trust Him with the outcome. Our disappointments are God's opportunities.

Allow Him to settle your heart, dry your tears and bring you through to the victory on the other side. But whatever you do, don't linger where there is no life.

John 10:10 'The thief comes only to kill, steal and destroy. I have come that you may have life, and life to the full'.

This is the plan that God has for us, He wants us to live a life that is full of blessing, full of the goodness that He has for us. So, if you find yourself sinking, call on God to bring you back to the place He wants you to be, and move out of disappointment and into the life of abundance that He has for you.

When a cloud of disappointment
Finds its way to your door
When heaviness surrounds you
And you can't take anymore.

When hurt has left you crippled
And your heart is held in pain
Tomorrow seems so pointless
Facing hardship all again.

It's then that Jesus holds you
And reminds you of His love
He sings over you His blessing
And whispers hope from up above.

He pours into you His promises
Of a life renewed by grace
And for your soul there is healing
As He wipes the tears from your face.

For this is just a moment
A short passageway in time
From the valley to the mountain
In the arms of the Divine.

In Due Season

Galatians 6:9 (ESV)

'And let us not grow weary of doing good, for in due season we will reap, if we do not give up'

Patience is not a word that any of us particularly like, however, there are some things in life that take time. Things that we are waiting for may not come in the timing that we would like them to, but they come in due season. This may not be today or tomorrow, but it will be when the time is right.

Just as the farmer plants his crops, he has to wait for the conditions to be right until he is able to eat what he has planted. In the same way, when a woman becomes pregnant, she waits nine months for the time when her baby is healthy and fully grown until she gives birth to him.

We live in a world that wants everything 'now'. We want the benefits without doing the hard yards. If we want something new but we can't afford it, we use Afterpay, if we want takeaway but can't be bothered going out, we get Uber Eats. Everything is available to us at the click of a finger, there is no reason to wait.

Yet, this scripture tells us that in 'due season' we will reap our reward if we don't give up.

Nothing that is truly precious, or worthy, is instantaneous. Some things take time, maybe a short time, or maybe longer than we would like, but if it's worth having what God has planned for us, then it's worth waiting for.

Sports stars don't just get up one morning and find they're amazing at what they do, it takes years of training to become truly great. Highly competitive and well-respected careers don't just happen, it takes a lot of work and years of study to be the best in your field.

Don't stop short or give up early in fulfilling God's plan for your life. Take the time that's needed for Him to grow you and develop you into what He's calling you to do or be.

You'll reap your harvest, a bountiful harvest - in due season

Lord walk with me through each season
And show me of your plan
Give me clear direction
And guide me by your hand.

Let me not rush ahead of you
But to stay within your will
That I would know your purpose
And in you would be filled.

Show me where I'm going
And the steps I'll need to take
And then go there before me
So there's no chance for mistakes.

As I wait patiently for your leading
And the whisper of your call
I will trust you in the middle
And offer you my all.

For in due season you will take me
To the door that I'll walk through
But while I wait in the hallway
I will bring all my praises unto you.

His Direction

Proverbs 3:5-6 (NIV)
'Trust in the Lord with all your heart, and lean not on your own understanding; in all your ways acknowledge Him, and He shall direct your paths'

It's not always easy trusting in the great unknown. To leave the fate of your life in the hands of someone else, hoping that it all turns out for the best. It can be difficult to just live in the moment and believe that tomorrow will be ok.

However, God calls us to trust in Him with all of our heart, not just some of it. To wholeheartedly hand over every part of who we are, what we dream of, and what we're planning for, to Him. He instructs us to not lean on our own understanding, but to acknowledge Him in all our ways.

This doesn't mean we just trust Him on the good days, the days when our lives are going well, and our world is at peace. It means that even when it's hard, when we don't know what's going on, when we're lost and adrift, that we continue to acknowledge Him, trust Him, and lean on Him.

In doing this, we shall reap the ultimate benefit that is written in the last part of this verse - that He will direct our paths.

There is nothing better than knowing that God goes before us, leading us and directing us in the way He would have us to go. He will open doors and bring us into places that no amount of trying on our part could bring us to, yet when we walk with God, He makes the impossible, possible.

My prayer for you today is that your heart would trust in God, that you would lean on Him, acknowledge Him in all your ways, and allow Him to direct your paths.

Lord help me to follow after you
And know which path to take
That I would walk in your leading
In every decision that I make.

May my mind be fixed upon you
as you direct my way
as I trust in your calling
and follow after you each day.

Let my hope be in you alone
As I face what is ahead
And let my gaze be fixed on you
As by your spirit I am led.

Show me your plan and purpose
That my vision would increase
That I would know your will for me
And all my anxiety would cease.

Lord I place my trust in your direction
And follow where you call
As in faith I walk towards you
And give to you my all.

Gracious Love of God

Psalm 139:9-10 (GNT)

'If I flew away beyond the east, or lived in the farthest place in the west, You would be there to lead me, You would be there to help me'

There is no where we can go that we are lost from God. No amount of running or hiding will remove us from Him. He knew us before we were born, He chose us, and He loves us. No matter what we do, say or think, His heart will always be for us.

The prodigal can never outrun God, they can never find a place to hide that His love wouldn't seek them out. No matter what choices they have made, or what their lifestyle may look like, God will still go after them. Like the one lost sheep, God will never give up looking for just that one, until He has them safely back with Him in the flock. If you are the parent of a prodigal child, remember, God loves them far more than you do, and He will go to the ends of the earth to bring them back home to Himself again.

In a world of throw away love, or performance and work-based love, it can be hard to fathom that God's love for us has nothing to do with what we do or don't do, but everything to do with what He has done for us.

It is so reassuring to know that we don't have to strive for perfection, or need to earn the love of God, all we need to do is accept Him and all that He has for us.

So today I would pray that you would find yourself in a place of complete surrender to the gracious love of God, that you wouldn't run or hide from all that He has for you, but you would open your arms and your heart to the all-consuming love of Christ and find your peace and hope in Him.

I feel your love in the early morning
When the day begins anew
When I walk and rise in peacefulness
And clothe myself in your truth.

I feel your love as the day is ending
And my world feels complete
When I am surrounded by your goodness
And lay my burdens at your feet.

I feel your love in the midst of sorrow
When tears are more than smiles
When you cover me with kindness
And embrace me as your child.

I feel your love during devastation
When all my dreams are lost
When my head is bowed in silence
And my heart bears the cost.

For in all things I know you love me
And your care for me is great
I thank you God for your faithfulness
And your everlasting grace.

Fear Not

Deuteronomy 31:6 (TLB)

'Be strong! Be courageous! Do not be afraid of them! For the Lord your God will be with you. He will neither fail you nor forsake you'.

We all go through situations in our lives where we are afraid and fearful. We lack courage to face what is before us, we doubt that we can make it through, or that we will be strong enough to face whatever battle is ahead.

As parents we worry for our children, what the future will hold for them, the consequences of their decisions, their safety and well-being. For ourselves we worry about our jobs, our health, our ability to have an income and provide for those in our care.

There are so many things that take our focus off Jesus, and have us lying awake at night, fearful for how we will face the next day, and the weeks ahead.

But we are instructed not to fear, but to know that the Lord is going with us, and He will not take His help away from us. He is with us on our journey, so He encourages us to be courageous, to not be discouraged by that which makes us fearful, but to push through, trusting in Him.

This is such a beautiful promise, we are not being left alone to deal with the storms of life by ourselves, but we have God beside us each step of the way. He doesn't leave us alone in our fear, our anxiety, or our panic, but He continues to walk with us. He goes before us to ensure the path ahead is safe for us, and He has His angels surrounding us, protecting us at the back and at the front.

Whatever is holding you captive, let it go. Let your courage be greater that your fear, and let God be the one you cling to, your safe place, and your anchor in the storm.

When I'm crippled by my feelings
And held prisoner by my fear
I come before you with shaking
And trust that you'll come near.

I am desperate for your healing
From all that holds me down
I need you to walk beside me
That in you my faith may abound.

Lord give me courage for tomorrow
And hope for today
That I would have peace within my body
And on you my thoughts would stay.

Let me walk with you in confidence
And know you have a plan
That there is purpose in my future
And that I will boldly stand.

I thank you God for your goodness
And your overwhelming care
That though I walk through the shadow
I'm not alone, for you are there.

Give Thanks

1 Thessalonians 5:18 (NIV)
'Give thanks in all circumstances, for this is God's will for you in Christ Jesus'

We are encouraged to be thankful in all circumstances.

This is not a chore when all is going well, when we have good health, great relationships with family and friends, a roof over our head, and a job that is rewarding. However, when all is not well, then it's certainly not easy to be thankful. Especially when life is difficult, when the road ahead looks uncertain, and when we are faced with disappointment.

However, our call is to be thankful 'IN' all circumstances, not because of our circumstance.

Jesus knew only too well what it was like to be faced with difficult and painful situations, yet at all times, He kept His eyes firmly on His Father, and on the bigger picture. He chose to be grateful, even when He had no reason to be.

We all face moments in life that are unbearable, but none of us has ever faced anything like Jesus did when He suffered on the cross. In His darkest moments, He knew that He was fulfilling the will of the Father, and therefore He was able to face the unbelievable pain and suffering He was to endure. Jesus wasn't thankful for His situation, but He chose to remain thankful in His situation.

Thankfulness is not just words that we express, but rather it is an attitude of our heart. It is the knowledge that no matter what today holds, that we can be grateful to the one who holds us.

So, whether you are currently facing a season that is difficult and painful, or if you have made it to the mountain top, give thanks 'IN' all things.

God is still good, on your great days and on your worst days, He is worthy of all our thankfulness, from hearts that are grateful.

With gratefulness I thank you
For all that you have done
Every gift that you have given
For the work you have begun.

I'm overcome by your riches
And the blessings you bestow
You bathe me with your kindness
And my cup it overflows.

When I'm lost at sea and sinking
Your hand it draws me near
You keep my head above the water
And remove from me all fear.

On days when I might doubt you
You remind me of who you are
The God of every miracle
My bright and shining star.

You're my portion in all circumstance
My Saviour and my friend
The one who is closer than a brother
The beginning and the end.

Changed by Christ

Romans 12:2 (GW)

'Don't become like the people of this world. Instead, change the way you think. Then you will be able to determine what God really wants, what is good, pleasing, and perfect'

Every day we are surrounded by people who bring us down, who are negative, and who see life through a glass half empty. They can be people we work with, live with or choose to spend our time with. However, just because we are surrounded by these people, doesn't mean we need to act or behave like them.

God's Word tells us not to change to be like the people of this world, but that we are to have a new way of thinking, that we need our thought life to come under submission to Him.

We don't need to bring ourselves down to the level of those around us, in our behaviour, our actions or our speech, but we are to always stay in an attitude of reverence to God and allow Him to be the focus of our being.

It is so easy to be swayed by those we spend the majority of our time with, but our mission should be that we sway them rather than the other way around. Our goal should be to bring positivity into negative situations, offer truth when we are surrounded by deceit, and let the light of God shine in the dark places.

Today I would encourage you, not to get caught up in the drama of others, don't fall into the trap of joining in with what you know in your heart is wrong, and don't be fooled by thinking it's only a little thing and it doesn't matter.

Everything matters.

Let Jesus take hold of your thoughts, and let Him change you from the inside out, that you may go out and change the world for Him.

Lord you call me to be different
From all those that I see
You want me to make a difference
That captives may walk free.

You've called me for a purpose
And my life has a plan
I need to walk above the water
Not stay stuck within the sand.

You've given me a mission
That my life would shine a light
So those in the darkness
Would be drawn out of the night.

You wash me with your words of truth
That I would boldly stand
And you walk with me to victory
As you hold up my weary hands.

My God I thank you for the strength you give
That my life would shine for you
That those around me would hear your voice
And be brought into your truth.

For Every Season

Ecclesiastes 3:1 (NIV)
'There is a time for everything, and a season for every activity under the heavens'

At the end of each year, or each season in our lives, we tend to look back and think through what took place, what things happened that were good, or what we would rather forget.

We can focus on the negatives, or we can thank God for all that He provided for us, and for the way He sustained us during our difficult season. It's not always easy to be grateful or thankful in the hard times, but sometimes this is where the greatest growth takes place. The difficult days are the ones where we have to make a conscious decision to keep our head up, to keep going, to keep pressing in, and keep trusting in God. It's when we dig deep in our hard season, that we grow and bloom in the season that God has prepared us for.

Ecclesiastes 3 points out all the various seasons of life, the good and the bad. The beautiful things that we can glean from this are the promises of birth, of healing, of embracing, of mending, of love and of peace.

That even in the times when we are overwhelmed by sadness, or hurt, or loneliness, or even rejection, that God is still good.

Today I would encourage you to find the rainbow in your storm, to look above rather than below, and to find the joy in life when the thief has tried to steal all that you cling to. Don't allow your season to define who you are, but rather take from it any lessons you may have learnt, and let the rest go.

Choose today to give God the glory regardless of the circumstance, and to remain grateful for all that He has carried you through.

The magnificence of colour
As autumn leaves begin to change
Shining out your glory
As heaven declares your name

The beauty of the seasons
Your presence all around
No need to search endlessly
For in all things you are found

We see you in each sunset
And as the rainbow fills the sky
In the storm that surrounds us
And in the clouds rolling by

When daylight turns to darkness
The stars shine in the night
So still we see your power
As you guide us by your light

You are everywhere around us
All creation is your throne
So to you we give all honour
And we worship you alone

Be Set Free

John 8:32 (NIV)

'Then you will know the truth, and the truth will set you free'

The dictionary defines truth as 'that which is true or in accordance with fact or reality'.

At times in our lives, we all believe things to be true based on our perception of them, not necessarily an actual fact.

Truth brings about freedom, it allows us to live uncluttered lives, not weighed down by lies or deceptions.

Unfortunately, there are many lies that we sometimes buy into. We look in the mirror and believe that God should of or could have done something better with how we look. We see our friends and our neighbours, and we believe that their lives are so much better or more fruitful than ours. We think that if we had more money, we would be happier, or that if our partner or children changed their behaviour, our lives would suddenly be perfect.

None of these things are true, these are just smoke and mirrors to deceive us into thinking that everyone is doing so much better than us, and our lives are wasted or even ruined.

God's Word tells us that truth will set us free, it won't bring us under condemnation, it won't cause us to covet those around us, it won't have us playing the comparison game, it will set us free.

Freedom comes from believing what God says about us, and His great love for us. He cares for us individually just as we are. He never made a mistake with how we look, He never planned for us to be like the person next door, and He never expected that we, or our families, would be perfect.

My prayer for you is that you would drown out the lies that are trying to steal all that God came to give you, let His truth permeate your soul, and fill you with hope, knowing that you can walk in freedom as you walk in truth with Him.

There is freedom in the knowing
That your Word is the truth
That I can trust you in all things
I will not be shaken, nor moved.

There is peace that fills my being
From knowing who you are
And that you are with me
From you I never stray too far.

I'm held within your protection
And wrapped tenderly in love
Watched over and delighted in
From my Father up above.

Your words can be trusted
And your spirit holds me tight
As I continue to walk with you
And be led by your light.

I am grateful for your goodness
Your mercy and your grace
As your truth brings me freedom
and I'm held in your embrace.

The Good Shepherd

Psalm 23:2 (ESV)

'He makes me lie down in green pastures, He leads me beside still waters'

This is such a beautiful passage in the Psalms, it speaks of the kindness and love of God, how He gently takes us to where He would like us to go. He doesn't push us, He doesn't drag us, and He doesn't pull us, but He leads us.

Jesus, the good shepherd goes before us, He gently leads us, while all along He is preparing the path for us, clearing the space before us and making a way.

Sometimes we overlook the message in this verse, we can focus on the still waters, and lose sight of the leading. The shepherd always takes care of his sheep, he leads them to safety, to places of rest, to areas of provision. He never lets them just wander around aimlessly, without food, without rest and without purpose. He is always ensuring that they are taken care of, and if even one wanders away, the shepherd will leave all the others, to go and find that one lost sheep.

This is the same for us, our good shepherd leads us and takes care of us. His eye is always on us, and He always wants what's best for us.

However, God will not drag us to where we need to be, He will never force us to go anywhere, but He will always just gently lead, taking us on a journey that He has planned for us in advance. And on that journey, He will lead us to places that are good for us, that will refresh our souls, that will be a healing balm to our weary bones.

In your wanderings this week, know that Jesus, the ultimate good shepherd goes before us, and gently leads us along the path that He has prepared for us.

Follow after Him with a heart of gratefulness and praise knowing that He is leading you with love.

I feel you gently lead me
Where my feet are scared to go
But you take my hand my hand so lovingly
Into the land where I can grow.

I trust you with my everything
Although at times I doubt
Like a boat tossed on the water
Moved by waves in and out.

I commit to you my future
And your purpose I desire
But still I tread so carefully
With feet entrenched in mire.

Lord you fill me with your goodness
And my cup it overflows
So, help me walk with confidence
In a place that I don't know.

For my faith lies in your promise
That I am covered on all sides
I surrender all I cling to
And trust you God as my guide.

Battle of The Mind

Philippians 4:8 (NIV)

'Finally, brothers and sisters, whatever is true, whatever is noble, whatever is right, whatever is pure, whatever is lovely, whatever is admirable—if anything is excellent or praiseworthy—think about such things'

This verse is such a great example for the way we should live life. Instead of focusing on the negative, waiting on the disappointment, or always expecting the worst, we are encouraged to think about, to ponder on, and to move into a thought pattern built on truth.

The mind is an incredibly powerful tool, and it can be used to build us up, or tear us down, it all depends on our perspective and thought patterns. Our mind is the first place that the devil will attack for he knows that once he can get you believing his lies, then it's easy to drag you down into poor thinking, and from there, into making bad choices.

We all face times of despondency or anxiety. Times when our thoughts are scattered and can be irrational; built on fear, or doubt or hopelessness. But this shouldn't be our 'normal' way of thinking, we need to train ourselves to move away from this, and bring our thoughts into submission, and under the authority of the Holy Spirit.

When in the natural we may allow our mind to tell us we are unloved, the truth is God loves us; when we are overwhelmed by fear, the truth is God is with us in all situations; and when we doubt there is a hope for our future, the truth is God has a plan for us. It's when we shift our mindset from the negative, and allow what is pure, right and lovely to become our focus, that we are then able to move forward into God's truth.

Today let there be a shift in your thinking, align yourself with the Word of God, and fix your thoughts on all that is excellent and praiseworthy, for this is how we win the battle for our mind.

When all around me is unstable
And I know not where to go
I will cling to your promises
And hold tight to what I know.

When the dark night hides the sunshine
And fear consumes my soul
I will stand constant in my praying
For only you can make me whole.

When I'm surrounded by decisions
And struggle with my choice
I will trust in your wisdom
And respond only to your voice.

When doubting clouds my vision
And my dreams are filled with tears
I will lean on your understanding
For my heart you fill with cheer.

Lord you're my all in every circumstance
And you lead where I should go
You watch over me with kindness
And your great love to me you show.

So, I trust you in the hard times
And give thanks when times are good
For in all things you surround me
As you promised that you would.

Never Forsaken

Matthew 27:46 (NIV)
"My God, my God, why have you forsaken me?"

How often has this been the cry of each of our hearts? When we've felt forgotten, or alone; downcast and disappointed.

Just like Jesus, we have cried out to God wanting to know why He isn't moving on our behalf, why He isn't coming to our rescue and fixing our problems.

It's hard not to be despondent when we've been overlooked, when someone else gets the job we wanted, when our friends and family are better off than us financially, when our healing hasn't come, or when our relationships break down. It's in these times we want to know where God is and why He isn't helping us.

We can only imagine how Jesus felt during His time of need. He was hanging on a cross, beaten and covered in blood, and He cried to His Father in agony asking the same question that we all ask, "Where are you and why have you forgotten me?".

We know, from reading the scriptures, that God had never forgotten His son, but there was a bigger picture involved, and because of that, Jesus had to die, but it broke the Father's heart.

The truth for each of us is that God has not forgotten us, and we have never been abandoned, but there is always a bigger picture at work. God may not come to our rescue immediately, because there may be further lessons for us to learn. He may not answer us in the way we hope, and this could be for our own good. But God has never, and will never, forsake us. He loves us far too much for that.

So, be encouraged today in the knowledge that God will never abandon you or leave you in your broken state. He loves you with a never-ending love, and He is with you always.

As God watches over the sparrow
How much more over me?
For in my life He finds great value
And He desires to set me free.

He made me for enjoyment
To live and love each day
He delights in me always
And leads me along the way.

To Him I hold great value
A beautiful shining star
He created me like a diamond
As He shaped, then held my heart.

He gazes upon me with pleasure
As I bring glory to His name
For its here we walk in unison
As He ignites my faith in flames.

I will never take for granted
His precious love over me
He is my greatest treasure
And in Him I am redeemed.

Live in Peace with All

Romans 12:18 (NLT)

'Do all that you can to live in peace with everyone'

Like so many verses in the Bible, this can sometimes prove to be so much easier said than done.

No matter how hard we try, it seems to be near impossible to please all the people all the time. Most of us face times when we go through difficulties with others. It can be family members, friends, those in authority, work colleagues and even random people we meet throughout our day.

Although the christian 'ideal' is to let others see Christ in us, sometimes they get to see a little less of this, and a whole lot more of someone else.

Let's face it, some people can be downright prickly. They can be easily agitated and hard to get along with, and it would seem that everything we say or do might set them off on a tangent, that leaves us in the firing line.

Even Jesus was faced with people who caused Him angst, who picked on everything He did, who went out of their way to cause Him harm and distress. Yet throughout all His dealings with others, He continued to show love, kindness and forgiveness.

This is our benchmark for living in peace with everyone. No matter the situation, even when we are wrongly accused, when we are placed in positions where we are ridiculed and put down, where we are right and they are wrong, our response requires us to show the love of Jesus.

It's not easy, and it's not always going to be the choice we want to make, many times we'll want to fight back and retaliate, however, we are called to love and to forgive.

So, as you go about your week, let Christ reign in your heart and in your mind, and in all your dealings with others, as best you can, live in peace.

Lord teach me to love others
In the same way as you
That I might be a beacon
Of your goodness and your truth.

May I carry your peace within me
And may my life shine your light
Surrounded by your kindness
Empowered by your might.

Fill my heart with love unending
That I may show your grace
Let your spirit fill my being
As those around me I embrace.

May my cup be running over
So, my hands can reach out and care
For the lost sheep that surround me
The broken-hearted everywhere.

So, Lord I ask for your favour
That I may touch the world for you
Let me be your hands and heart to those
Who need to know your truth.

Live Life Well

Psalm 27:13 (NIV)
'I remain confident of this, I will see the goodness of the Lord in the land of the living'

Each of us has been given the same amount of time in our day, but not all of us have been given the same number of days.

We will never know when it is our time to go home and be with Jesus, and therefore, what we do with our time on earth is so incredibly important.

Some people are early risers, others are at their best at night, and for some like me, mid-morning to mid-afternoon is the optimal time of the day. But no matter when the best time for you is, we all know that we will need to give an account for how we've spent our time.

I think that as we get older, we tend to reflect more on what we do with our day, what we enjoyed, what we would change, who we spent time with, and what, if any, value did we add to the lives of others.

One day, for the majority, a eulogy will be spoken in regard to the life we have lived. The impact of that eulogy will depend on what you and I do today, and whom we may have touched on our journey.

I'm quite sure the aim for all of us is to reflect love not hate, compassion not apathy, forgiveness not bitterness, and most of all we want to shine the love of Jesus.

As you go about your day, look for opportunities to be a blessing, go out of your way to make someone feel special, pray with or over someone, do something that says, "Jesus lives in me", without actually saying anything at all.

Let's make the most of the time we have been given, and let us always remember to give thanks to God, and to give Him our very best in the time we have.

Let me see you in the morning
With the first ray of light
Let me hear you in the evening
When the dawn gives way to night.

Let my ears be ever open
To hear your voice call my name
That I will follow in your leading
and be forever changed.

Let my heart hear your whisper
Your promise in the dark
That your grace goes before me
And we will never be apart.

Let me be still in your presence
As your word engulfs my soul
My life I give to you Lord Jesus
The only one who makes me whole.

In every moment may I know you
And feel your presence all around
That I may live my days in worship
And my love for you will abound.

Stretch Your Faith

Matthew 12:13 (NIV)

'Then he said to the man, "Stretch out your hand." So, he stretched it out and it was completely restored, just as sound as the other'

Each of us is looking for a touch from Jesus, whether it be physical healing, healing from hurt, or even healing from painful memories; we want a real and tangible touch from Him.

Sometimes we think that our role in the healing is to just wait, to sit back and to trust God for a good outcome.

But we notice in this scripture that Jesus tells the man to 'stretch out his hand'. There was a doing on his part. He wasn't told to go away and pray more, he wasn't told to be patient and wait, he wasn't told to just have faith, but he was told to physically do something.

There will be times in each of our lives when something is expected of us, when we need to reach out to God, we need to take a step of faith, and we need to bring every part of us to Jesus.

This man could have been healed just by a simple prayer, or a look, or with the words 'Your faith has healed you', but Jesus didn't choose to do it for him in this way, He asked him to make the first move, He asked the man to 'stretch out his hand'. It was a partnership between Jesus and the man, Jesus would give him his healing, but first he had to do his part.

If you find yourself in a place where healing hasn't come yet, stretch your faith, place your petition at the feet of Jesus, move forward toward Him, and continue to trust for complete restoration within your body, soul and spirit.

Take that leap of faith, and stretch out your hand to Jesus, allowing Him to reach out and touch you, right where you are.

I would encourage you today to partner with Him, to never give up believing, and to be prepared for whatever He calls you to do.

As I wait on you for healing
Give me faith to trust each day
To know you walk beside me
And your Word has the last say.

I won't bow down to deception
To give in to fear and doubt
But I will reach out to you with both hands
Knowing you will see this out.

For it's when I lean into your faithfulness
And believe you'll bring me through
That my hope is lifted higher
And my gaze is set on you.

In you Lord is my restoration
Both in body and in soul
You are my strong tower
The only one who makes me whole.

So I place my life into your hands Lord
And trust wholly in your care
For in you God there is healing
And this would be my prayer.

Pure and Steadfast

Psalm 51:10 (NIV)

'Create in me a pure heart, O God, and renew a steadfast spirit within me'

According to the dictionary the word pure means 'clean or spotless', and the word steadfast means to be 'firm and unwavering'.

In this scripture, David is asking God to give him a heart that is without blemish, and a spirit that remains strong and unmoveable. These are such beautiful attributes to have, that we may be whole and acceptable in the sight of God. But a heart that is pure requires a lot of cleansing. There is no room for deceit, idolatry, jealousy, bitterness, gossip, or hate. In the natural there is no way we can make this happen; to remove all the ugliness in our hearts we need the help of God and the Holy Spirit to cleanse us. We live in a world that is fallen, and therefore we can be consumed by the underlying darkness that is all around us, which can then permeate into us. God in His goodness can replace what has been fed into our hearts that is not from Him, He can strip out the ugly, and replace it with beauty, all we need to do is ask.

David then goes on to ask for a renewed steadfast spirit.

This is something we all need. We need to stand firm and unwavering in our faith, in our belief, our hopes and dreams. We need to be able to withstand all that is thrown at us, so that we may remain upright, and that we would continue to place our trust in God. It's not easy to be steadfast when life is hard, when things don't work out the way we thought they would, or when our hope becomes battered, and this is why we need God to continually renew a steadfast spirit within us, so that in all situations and circumstances we can remain firm.

I encourage you today to make this your prayer, that God would give you a heart that is clean, and a spirit that is unwavering, that you might live your life fully acceptable to Him.

Lord I fall upon your mercy
And cry out for your embrace
My soul seeks restoration
And the kindness of your grace

I come before you a sinner
Who can no longer walk alone
I ask for your forgiveness
As I kneel before your throne

I hand to you my weakness
And all I harbour in my heart
I commit to you my wanderings
And all the darkness from my past

I choose you above all others
As I offer up my praise
I rise up in my salvation
To give you honour all my days

Lord create in me a pure heart
As I bow before you my King
And renew again my spirit
That my soul to you might sing.

Open Doors

Matthew 7:7 (NIV)
'Ask and it will be given to you; seek and you will find; knock and the door will be opened to you'

Sometimes when we stand at a closed door, we think we've reached the end, we think this is the final answer and we can go no further. Sometimes the door represents things in our life that we think we need, maybe a job, or a relationship, and we can't possibly understand why God would allow the door to stay closed when we think this is the best thing for us.

However, for our own benefit or good God will allow doors to stay closed for a longer season, if He thinks that might be necessary. He can see the path ahead of us, and He knows whether an open door right now would cause us more harm or pain, than if we waited a bit longer. We all know that waiting can be hard, it can seem to take forever when we are desperate for change or we're longing for an improvement in our situation, but while we wait, God is there for us. He is staying the course with us and encouraging us as we get closer to that which we'd hoped for.

Sometimes we feel that if the door isn't opening, then God must be punishing us, or just choosing to withhold from us something that we want, but that is never the case. God will never open doors for us that will cause us more harm than good, He loves us far too much for that.

But in the right time, doors will open. These may not be the doors that we had originally hoped for, but God may open bigger and better doors, doors that will lead to great adventures, amazing opportunities, and to places we had never expected.

Whatever door you're waiting for God to open, trust Him in the interim and know that He isn't making you wait to hurt you, but because He loves you. I pray that whatever door you're standing in front of, God would open it in His perfect time.

As I stand before a closing door
Lord I trust you once again
And know that you walk with me
And will stay until the end.

Though I am filled with disappointment
In you I place my trust
I lean not on my own understanding
But know my faith in you is a must.

I wait upon your timing
Knowing you always have a plan
And though the door's not open
I choose in faith to stand.

I seek you with my whole heart
And hope wholly in your Word
For you are the God of promises
And I know my cries you have heard.

So as I wait for an opening
To cross through to the other side
I will trust only in you Jesus
My refuge and my guide.

I Entrust My Life to You

Psalm 143:8 (NIV)

'Let the morning bring me word of your unfailing love, for I have put my trust in you. Show me the way I should go, for to you I entrust my life'

This beautiful prayer of David in the Psalms should be the cry of each of our hearts. That we would desire God's unfailing love, put our trust in Him, that we would seek His direction, and that we would entrust our lives to Him.

Of the many areas we struggle with, it would seem that entrusting our lives to God is one of the most difficult. It is about learning to let go of control and allowing God to do in us and for us, far above all we ever hoped or dreamed.

So often, we hold on tightly to every aspect of our lives. We are terrified to let go of anything, just in case it all falls apart. We feel that if we direct everything that is going on within us and around us, then all should go smoothly.

Yet, we have found time and time again, this just is not the case. We don't allow for all the things that can happen in life that we are not prepared for. We may face illness, retrenchments, abandonment, financial loss, or heartbreak. There are so many things we can't control, and yet we still struggle to entrust our lives to the very one who takes care of us.

We are promised that God will be with us always, that He will never leave us or forsake us, and we know that He loves us with an everlasting love. These things alone should be enough to fill us with hope and confidence. They should speak to our soul and whisper deep into our heart that we are cherished, provided for, and being led into all that God has prepared for us.

My encouragement for you today is that you would continue to entrust your life to God, that you would rely on His unfailing love for you, and that you would place your trust in Him and His direction for your life.

Lord with all I am I trust you
And walk within your ways
I will follow where you lead me
And love you all my days.

I will look for you each morning
And will lavish in your love
Believing that I'm cherished
By the one true God above.

I know you have a plan for me
A purpose in what I do
So I will place all my hope in you
And rest in your truth.

I entrust my life to your calling
Knowing you direct my path
So on you I keep my focus
My soul finds peace at last.

In all ways I will seek you
And let go of my control
I trust you in every circumstance
For it's you who makes me whole.

No Greater Love

John 3:16 (NIV)

'For God so loved the world that He gave His one and only son…'

Every year in February a day is set aside to celebrate love, this is Valentine's Day. A day that is primarily for couples to express and show their love for each other. It is a day when the modern world is over-run with commercialism. When love is shown by the purchasing of flowers, chocolates, jewellery and meals. It is known to be one of the biggest days of the year for couples to become engaged.

However, love is more than just couples, and it is celebrated on more than just one day each year. There is the love between a parent and their child, the love between siblings, and the love between friends.

Yet more importantly, there is the love that is shared between God and us. A love that transcends any concept that the world could ever understand. A love where God would give up His only son, in order that we might have the opportunity to come into a relationship with Him.

This love runs deeper than the relationship that we have with our significant other, and it is not just celebrated on one special day of the year, but it is a love of such unbelievable proportions, that it should in fact, be celebrated every day of the year.

Who else but God would sacrifice something of such huge significance for us? Who would be willing to allow their child to be born, and then to suffer an agonising death for the sake of an undeserving world?

This is the greatest love story, a monumental sacrifice, the deepest passion and the most beautiful hope of redemption. This is a love worth celebrating.

I would encourage you today to put aside some time to think on, and to be grateful for the precious love that God has for you, that He would give up His son, that you might have life.

As I cast my mind to Calvary
And the victory that you won
I stand in awe of your sacrifice
My Lord, God's chosen son.

That you would give your life for me
And die a brutal death
I've overwhelmed by your goodness
As I think on your last breath.

They beat you and they mocked you
Casting lots for your clothes
They treated you with violence
Right up to that final blow.

When you bowed your head in silence
To do your Father's will
The ground shook beneath you
Until the world around you was still.

I will always choose to be grateful
For the debt you paid for me
For my life you were the sacrifice
So, I give my life back to thee.

Serve God

Joshua 24:15 (AMP)

'Choose for yourselves this day whom you will serve….
as for me and my house, we will serve the Lord'

Every day we are bombarded with choices. From the time we open our eyes, until we go to bed, there are endless decisions to be made.

There are all the simple choices, such as what to have for breakfast, what to wear, or whether to go to the gym, and then there's the more complicated choices, university and careers, finding a marriage partner, buying a home, or whether to go to the mission field. We have so many decisions in our lives, some of these are easy and require no real thought, others require a deeper level of thinking, and in many cases, a great amount of prayer.

One choice that we are all given, is who we will serve. Will we make the decision to follow and serve God, or will we go the other way and follow and serve the devil?

To serve the devil, is in fact just another way of serving ourselves. By putting all of our desires before all else, we are choosing to ignore the bigger picture of what God has for us. We choose to give ourselves the highest honour, being self-seeking, looking for ways to have all our needs met, regardless of the cost.

The choice to serve God requires us to put ourselves last, and to put Him and others first. This isn't always an easy choice to make, yet we have the greatest example to follow. The life of Jesus was always about serving His Father, doing His will, and in that, He served us. We saw that when He washed the feet of the disciples that He was painting for us a beautiful picture of servanthood, and then when He went to the cross, it was so that we would have reconciliation with the Father.

So, I would encourage you today, choose wholeheartedly to serve the Lord, follow after Him, take on a servant heart, and let Him lead you into the calling He has for you. This is the greatest decision you could ever make.

As the dawn brings in a new day
And I choose whom I will serve
Lord I give you every moment
Holding nothing in reserve.

I will thank you in each season
And praise you though it's hard
In all things I'll be grateful
and offer up to you, my heart.

I will seek out your will for me
And walk within your ways
I will acknowledge you in all things
As I go with you through my day.

Let your word be a lamp to me
I pray my path you would light
Guiding me through the darkness
As you lead me to the other side.

So, as I begin my day with you
I choose to serve you alone
For you are Christ, my Redeemer
My Lord, my God, my home.

Well Done

Matthew 25:21 (NIV)
'Well done, good and faithful servant'

On the day when we go to meet Jesus, these are the words that we all want to hear. We want to hear Him say "well done" and to describe us as both good, and faithful.

What does it mean to be good? It can mean that we have been kind, we've shown compassion and mercy, we've provided for others, or even that we have sacrificed ourselves for the benefit of those around us.

We can be good, and we can do good. One is our nature, and the other our intention in action. God wants us to be both. It's not enough that we simply think about doing good for others, we need to intentionally outwork this, so that we provide hope and blessing, and therefore bring glory to God.

To be faithful requires from us discipline, and sacrifice. Showing faithfulness day after day can be difficult, it forces us to commit to a task and stick with it. It ensures that we stay the course, without wavering, and we endure regardless of the cost.

It is Jesus desire that we stay faithful to Him. He wants us to remain in Him, continually praying, reading His Word, and offering up praise. He requires that we are faithful to each other, loving one another, serving, honouring and encouraging.

And finally in this passage, we are called servants. A servant is one who does everything for the sake of another. Their entire life is to benefit those they serve, to choose to honour another more highly than themselves, to give, and then give some more.

My prayer for each of us, is that on the day we meet with our Saviour, that to each of us He says, "Well done good and faithful servant".

On the day I ascend to glory
This is my heartfelt prayer
That you would reach your hand to me
And I would stand before you there.

I long to hear these words of yours
That would say to me 'well done'
And I would walk forever
With the Father, Spirit, Son.

Lord let my life on earth be yours
That I would follow in your ways
That in all things I would seek you
And give you glory all my days.

Teach me to love others
And in all things to be kind
Let me live as your servant
So that true life I may find.

Prepare me Lord for eternity
For my meeting place with you
As I walk uprightly in your presence
And live only in your truth.

A Small Quiet Whisper

Matthew 11:15 (NIV)
'Whoever has ears, let them hear'

When my daughter was a little girl, to make sure she had my full attention, she would take both sides of my face in her little hands and have me look directly at her. This way she would know that there was nothing distracting me, and that I was actively listening to what she had to say.

I sometimes think that's the way it is with God, He wants to know that He has our full attention, that we are truly listening to what He is saying. In order for Him to get our attention, He sometimes allows situations to come into our lives to slow us down, make us stop, and have us turn our focus onto Him.

We live in a world that is filled with noise, with distractions, and with busyness, where the voice of God is easily drowned out. We are so busy going from one activity to another, that we miss the small quiet whisper that is God gently speaking to us.

We sometimes wonder why God is so distant when we are waiting for Him to answer us, yet quite often we don't stop long enough to listen for His voice.

If we truly want to hear from God, we need to take the time to listen. We need to rid ourselves of everything that is blocking us hearing His voice. This could mean turning off the tv, getting up earlier, lessening our time on social media, saying no to outside commitments. Whatever it is that is stopping us from hearing God's voice, these things need to be pushed aside, to make way for Him to be heard.

I would challenge you today to actively listen, to turn your full attention, to put away all distractions, and to allow God to whisper into your ears, into your mind, into your heart and into your soul all that He has for you.

Say no to the world and say yes to God, hear today what it is He wants to say to you.

When you whisper may I hear you
And come running to your voice
That I would live my life in surrender
That your will would be my choice.

May I fall down to you in worship
And bring glory to your name
That I would give up all worldly pleasures
And search only for your fame.

To be found within your presence
Where all else falls away
And I'm left in the arms of Jesus
The home where I would stay.

Let me be forever grateful
For all you give and so much more
For when I am touched by your spirit
My life becomes an open door.

Take me Lord into my calling
Into the plans you have for me
Where hope and peace become my anchor
And my soul can fly free.

Be Kind

Colossians 3:12 (NIV)

'Therefore, as God's chosen people, holy and dearly loved, clothe yourselves with compassion, kindness, humility, gentleness and patience'

There is a beautiful quote by Caroline Flack which says, "In a world where you can be anything, be kind".

What an excellent exhortation this is!

We are told every day that we can be anything we want, we can do whatever we put our minds to, we can have what we want if we work towards it. But all of those things, whatever we attain in life, wherever we go or whatever we do, they all mean nothing if we have chosen to be unkind to those around us.

Scripture tells us, that as God's chosen people, we are to clothe ourselves with, amongst other things, kindness. We need to be helpful towards others, we need to share and to give, we need to honour others, we need to be considerate and generous.

A kind person will always go out of their way to make others feel included and special, they will avoid conflict but instead speak with love. We live in a fallen world, and we are surrounded by selfishness, where everything is about self, rather than caring for those around us. But this is not the biblical way of doing life. God's people are about love, and grace, and hope, and friendship. This is the way Jesus lived His life, and it's the way we are expected to live ours. We are commanded to 'love others', we do this by showing them kindness.

Today I would encourage you to go out of your way to show kindness to those around you. Give love where it's undeserved, forgive even if it's hard, smile at someone you don't know, encourage those around you. No matter what you do, in any way possible, show the kindness of God to those you meet, for you it may be a simple thing, for them it could be life changing.

Therefore as God's chosen people
Let us clothe ourselves in love
That we would give to others
As an act of worship to the Lord above.

Let us always offer kindness
And show compassion to those in need
That in us they see Jesus
And in Him can be free.

May we walk uprightly and be humble
Being gentle to those we meet
For each one is in a battle
That we may never see.

Christ is our example
Of the life that we should lead
For love was His vocation
He cared for everyone in need.

So may we be filled with Godly kindness
And offer hope to all around
That our Lord may be glorified
And in His presence may we be found.

Mighty in Power

Joshua 3:13 (NLT)
'As soon as their feet touch the water, the flow of water will be cut off upstream, and the river will stand up like a wall'

Can you imagine what this must have been like? This miracle took place during harvest time, a time when the Jordan river was flooded, yet our God, mighty in power, stopped the flow of water to allow His people to cross over into the promised land.

There are times in our lives when we know God has a plan, but we have no idea how it will be executed. We look at our circumstances, and we find ourselves shrouded in fear and doubt, unsure of how to move forward or if God will provide a way out.

I'm sure when the Israelites looked at the water before them, they thought, once again, we are never going to reach our promise, we will never fulfil our potential, we will never have a home. Just like us, they would have seen the negative standing in front of them and they would have felt discouraged and without hope.

Yet God had a plan, it required Joshua to step out in faith, once again, and do something that looked crazy, that would seem totally unbelievable, and that could have had devastating consequences. But God stepped in! He did exactly what He said He would do. He parted the waters and led His people through on dry ground to the promised land.

If you find yourself standing on the wrong side of the river, if you're looking towards the future but can't seem to find your way there, or if your promise looks unreachable, keep trusting God. If He can stop the flow of water to allow an entire nation of people to cross the river, He can bring you into all He has for you.

I encourage you today to keep hoping, trusting and believing in the God of miracles. He's got your situation in hand, just hold onto Him, and be ready to move when He says it's time. Just as He was with the Israelites, so He is with you.

As I walk through the wilderness
I know I don't walk alone
For you go before me
As you prepare for me a home.

I will cross to my promised land
The place you have called me to be
A land of milk and honey
Where your goodness I will see.

You walk with me in the desert place
The barren and the dark
But I know this time is ending
From this journey I'll disembark.

I will soon cross the Jordan
Into all you have for me
And there I'll sing your praises
Of the way you set me free.

There is hope when all seems hopeless
I know my future you have planned
So, I'll trust you in my wilderness
And on your promises I'll stand.

Cherish God's Message

Psalm 119:143 (TPT)

'Even though my troubles overwhelm me with anguish, I still delight and cherish every message you speak to me'

This is just so beautifully written.

We can be in the midst of our darkest days, we can be surrounded by sorrow and disappointment, yet we can choose to still delight in and cherish each and every message that comes from God.

Sometimes it can be hard to see the light when you're walking through a difficult situation. It's almost impossible to see anything except your own problems, and you can feel completely overwhelmed by them. We can feel defeated and knocked down, with very little hope for the days to get better.

Yet God in His goodness is right there with us. Every word He speaks to us, each whisper into our heart, every little encouragement, is an absolute gift on the days and in the weeks when we are suffering.

When we are barely holding on, when our faith is something we cling to like a raft in a raging ocean, to hear the voice of God, that is the moment when we know that we are loved, and we are not alone.

There will always be hard times, we will all go through things that we feel like we may never recover from, we will all have hopes dashed and dreams lost. But, in the midst of that, God continues to speak to us, He continues to lead us, and most importantly, He continues to be our constant source of love.

Let me encourage you today, whatever your season, it is just that, a season. But know, that in the midst of what you're walking through, God is with you, whispering His promises into your heart. Cherish all that He is saying to you and hold tight to Him. In all things, let Him be your delight.

I cherish all that I have read
And all that I've been told
The stories of your faithfulness
Have been passed down from days of old.

Your provision in the days of need
Where loaves and fish became a feast
Where no one was left hungry
You fed the greatest and the least.

You led your people out of Egypt
And into the promised land
You walked with our fathers
And guided them with your hand.

You chose a girl from out of nowhere
To give birth to a king
You blessed her with a miracle
A spotless lamb without sin.

So, Lord I stand on your promises
Of the goodness I have heard
And I will trust you with my whole heart
And live only by your word.

Freely Give

Matthew 10:8 (NIV)
'Heal the sick, cleanse the lepers, raise the dead, cast out demons. Freely you have received, freely give'

Jesus, when He commissioned His disciples, gave them power to perform amazing miracles. He imparted to them the ability to do what only He had been able to do to that point. He was sending them into the world to take care of the sick, not just in body, but in mind and spirit. He reminded them that all that they had, and all that they needed, they had freely received, and therefore, they were to freely give.

This is for all of us, Jesus has, through the Holy Spirit, placed within each of us the power to pray into each and every situation of those around us.

Everything we have in life comes from our Heavenly Father; our good health, our sound minds, our rested spirit. He freely gives us the ability to get up each day, to earn a living, to enjoy our lives without great limitations. For the most part, we live lives of blessing. There was nothing we did to earn this, and nothing that we have received has been at any cost to us. Jesus has freely given us all that we have. Now it's up to us to freely give.

Jesus wants us to give all that we have, to share with others, to impart into the lives of those around us.

We are surrounded by people who are hurting; physically, mentally and spiritually. We are called to pray, to walk alongside people, to bless them financially, to love unconditionally, to open up our homes and be hospitable, and to lead them to Christ.

I would encourage you today to take stock of all that you have freely received, and then go out into your world, and freely give to those around you.

Remember, you are the hands and feet of Jesus, so go where He calls you, and bless those He puts on your path.

I'm in awe of all you promise
And the blessings that you give
You say that it's your pleasure
That in abundance I might live.

I have the benefits of your kingdom
And the rights as your heir
I'm dressed in royal garments
And have a throne as my chair.

All creation is for my enjoyment
You withhold no good gift
I'm surrounded by such beauty
So, my praise to you I give.

You are my Jehovah-Jireh
For you provide all I need
Your heart does not stop giving
Into my life your blessings feed.

So I give you all my gratefulness
And I offer you my all
Your love for me is overwhelming
My God of you I am in awe.

Our Daily Bread

Matthew 6:11 (AMP)
'Give us this day our daily bread'

The Lord's Prayer is something most of us who grew up in the church could quote quite easily. It tends to roll off our tongues without us giving it a lot of thought.

However, when it is broken down into smaller segments, the meaning behind the words become deeper and more intentional.

This portion of scripture is especially pointed in that it is directed at one moment of time – today. There is no mention of tomorrow, or next week, or next month, it only says today.

So often we get caught up in worrying about what tomorrow will hold, we totally lose sight of the fact that we need only take one day at a time. We miss the point that if God is providing for us today, then surely, He will provide for us again tomorrow. We are constantly concerned with having all our needs met, not just today, but next week, next month and even next year.

It seems that gone are the days of a simple life, where we were satisfied with what we had, and in that, whatever we had was enough. The days of not planning too far ahead are just a remnant of the past, of a life that most people struggle to remember.

We are now a generation of planners. We plan for our future, our children's future, our budgets, our holidays, our retirement, everything is planned for down to the last detail.

The endless amount of stress we cause ourselves by being on the treadmill of life that says 'more, more, more'. Yet, when we look around, we actually have more than enough. We have so much, yet we continue to worry if our daily bread will be provided for.

Today, take time out from your planning and sit in contentment. Trust that God will take care of you tomorrow, just as He has today. Give thanks that for this day He will give us our daily bread.

As His eye is on the sparrow
Know evermore it's on you
And as He watches with affection
He fills your life with His truth.

As He knows every grain of sand
He also knows your need
And the one who fed with loaves and fish
Your hungry soul will feed.

The birds worry not for tomorrow
For they know they're in His hand
If He can keep them close to Him
Then surely He'll help you stand.

So rest today in the knowledge
That the God of heaven hears your prayer
And even though just a whisper
He will not leave you in despair.

Hold tight to His promises
Trust in our God who cares
For you're worth more than the sparrow
And all your burdens He will bear.

Be Defined By Christ

---

2 Corinthians 5:17 (ESV)
'If anyone is in Christ he is a new creation, the old has passed away, behold the new has come'

So often we see people, ourselves included, define themselves by mistakes they have made. It's easy to fall into the 'if only' trap, where we can think, and even at times fully believe, that if we had only done something different, we would be in a better place. If we had chosen a different path, or different friends or career, or if we hadn't made that one mistake, our lives would be so much better.

What we don't realise is that what we sometimes see as mistakes, God sees as an opportunity to shine through us. God will take what we have done, or have been through, and use that as a platform for His own glory.

He doesn't define us by all the things we've done wrong, by the times we've messed up, or jumped headfirst into what He knew would be a disaster. He defines us by the finished work on the cross, that while we were still sinners Jesus died for us. His love for us was so great, that regardless of what we have done, He sent His only son to the cross for us.

Our past is just that, it's past. There is no going back and changing what took place, what we did or didn't do is gone, and all we can do now is move forward. Yet sometimes that can be the hardest part, the part where we need to forgive ourselves, let go of what took place, and move on. If God is not holding our past against us, then we certainly shouldn't be.

Today be encouraged by the fact that you are a new creation, that each morning God gives you new mercies, and all you need is to accept that mercy. Allow Him to lead you into the new life that He has for you, a life that is defined, not by your mistakes, but by His amazing love for you.

It's only in your grace and truth
That I stand unashamed
Washed clean in your perfect blood
And set free by your name.

I have no fear of tomorrow
Or concern for today
For I know who holds my future
So to you Lord I pray.

I need not doubt my salvation
For it's given by your grace
You see me through your eyes of love
When on the cross you took my place.

My faith is built on promises
The word of God is solid ground
And it's to your truth that I'm holding
And in your presence I am found.

For you stand before my accusers
And all the stones slip away
For all have sinned and fallen short
Only your grace will remain.

Do Not Be Anxious

Philippians 4:6 (ESV)

'Do not be anxious about anything, but in everything by prayer and supplication, with thanksgiving, let your requests be made known to God'

Each of us go through periods in our lives that are stressful. Whether we live with that stress for just a few hours, or whether it is with us for days, and possibly months, is all determined by what is going on around us, and how we manage that stress.

There are so many outside factors that bring about unrest in our lives, these can include work, finances, health, relationships, and fear.

It can also be said, that the more we worry about all the things that are going on in our lives, the worse the problems seem to get. We tend to focus solely on the situation, and it consumes us, making it hard to sleep, we can become sick, and we are overwhelmed with despair.

Yet, God in His goodness, wants us to place all of our anxiety on Him. His desire is that we would be anxious for nothing, but we would lay everything before Him. That includes the fear you face each morning, the worry over your wayward child, the unknown medical results, the broken relationship, the lost job, whatever it is you are suffering through, God wants to know about it.

Unlike us, God can see the beginning from the end, He knows exactly what is coming, and how the story will unfold. There is nothing that will be a surprise to Him, or throw Him off balance, therefore we can trust Him with our worry, our stress, and our concerns.

Let today be the day that you stop listening to the voices in your head that are leading you down a path of destruction. Take whatever is it that is controlling your mind and lay it at the feet of Jesus. He is more than able to handle all that you have going on, all you need to do is trust Him.

In the fire and the conflict
Where God's grace remains the same
Where He draws us to come closer
And find perspective once again.

When our hopes feel bruised and battered
And life has worn us down
It's there that He meets us
And His love for us abounds.

He reminds us of His promises
And instructs us in His truth
He encourages with His wisdom
And His favour is absolute.

As we walk through our valley
And climb out the other side
We sing a hallelujah
To our Lord God on high.

For He goes before us in the fire
And loves us in our pain
He promises His mercy
And He offers us His grace.

He Calms the Storm

Psalm 107:28-29 (NIV)
'Then they cried out to the Lord in their trouble, and He brought them out of their distress. He stilled the storm to a whisper; the waves of the sea were hushed'

Have you ever noticed the way a baby stops crying when their mother whispers gently in their ear? How when she holds the little one close to her and gently rocks her child, the crying subsides, and the tiny body calms itself.

This is what God does for us, His tender love, His gentle whisper, and His soothing breath of life calms us during the storm. Whatever it is in life that we may be facing, God is in the midst of it with us, He is surrounding us with His love, His peace, and His protection.

God wants us to cry out to Him, He wants us to know that He is with us in our distress and our trouble, that when we are surrounded by the storms of life, and when we think that the waves will consume us and take us under, that He is the God who can still the storm.

We can take comfort in knowing, that if God can calm a raging sea, if He can still a storm by just a whisper of His voice, then He is more than capable of being with us during the hardships in our lives. There is absolutely nothing that is too hard for God, there is no mountain that He can't move, and no sea that He can't part. All we need to do during our moments of distress is call out to Him, He will do the rest.

Today, allow God to whisper into your heart, allow Him to still the storm that is either raging within you or surrounding you. Don't give in to the waves that would try to drown you but hold tightly to His hand as He brings you to a place of safety and hope.

Trust in the whisper, hold tight to the promise, and believe in His truth.

I know it only takes a whisper
And the waves will fall away
Just one word from you Jesus
And peace can fill my day.

When I trust you in the battle
You go before me in the fight
All I need is to hold onto you
To see your power and your might.

You still the storm that surrounds me
And you're attentive to my need
In prayer you hear me crying
And my hungry soul you feed.

For when I lean into your promises
And focus only on your face
It's then that you cover me
With your peace, love and grace.

For in the storms that consume us
Your truth remains the same
You are our hope and our deliver
Jesus Christ the only name.

Jesus is The Vine

John 15:5 (NIV)

'I am the vine and you are the branches. If you remain in me, and I in you, you will bear much fruit; apart from me you can do nothing'

Jesus always told stories to describe situations, to make it easy for us to understand Him, and our relationship with Him. In this story He is the vine, and we are the branches that come off that vine, and He is telling us that in order for our lives to flourish, we need to stay attached to Him, who is our living source.

When branches fall from a tree, their beautiful leaves wither up, go crunchy and die. There is no longer any opportunity for them to grow or to produce fruit. This is how it can be with us, while we stay close and attached to Jesus we are nurtured and fed, enabling us to grow and to produce, but as soon as we pull back or fall away, things start to change. What was once beautiful and strong, and had a lingering sweet smell, becomes weak, frail and pungent.

There is no possible way for a branch to live a productive life without the vine, the branch always needs to stay attached. The vine will always continue to grow and sprout, but the branch has no hope unless it stays grafted to the very thing that gives it life.

Jesus, as the vine, is the giver of life to us. He takes care of us, tends mercifully towards us, and helps us to grow and become beautiful. At no point does the vine ever say to the branch 'I don't want you', but instead it always holds tight to it, and provides the perfect environment for the branch to stay whole and healthy.

Today, remember that you are the branch, and that your source of life comes from Jesus. Cling to the promise that if you remain grafted to Him, then you will bear much fruit, and live a good and productive life.

May my life be ever fruitful
And flourish under you
As I stay grafted to your promises
And held tightly by your truth.

Lord I pray my leaves don't wither
And die upon the ground
But let me bud in springtime
And in you always be found.

I pray that you would always nurture
And help me to grow
That I would be productive
And would reap that which I sow.

May my leaves be filled with fragrance
That others would find sweet
That they would be drawn to your vineyard
And in you be made complete.

I will stay close to you Jesus
As I hold tightly to the vine
For you are my hope and my provider
To you my life is entwined.

A Thankful Heart

1 Chronicles 16:34 (NIV)
'Oh give thanks to the Lord, for He is good, for His steadfast love endures forever'

There is nothing we can do that will ever be enough to show or tell the Lord how much we love Him, how much we appreciate His sacrifice, and how indebted we are to Him for His unwavering love for us.

The dictionary describes being grateful as 'warmly or deeply appreciative of benefits received'.

The benefits that we have received from our Saviour are too many to count, the way He blesses us far surpasses anything we deserve or could even imagine. We live lives of abundance only because of His goodness towards us.

When we live our lives filled with gratitude, it changes the way we see things around us, it gives us a new perspective and a better outlook. When we choose to focus on all that is good, rather than that which is bad, when we have a glass half full attitude, when we look at the world through rose coloured glasses, it allows us to have a happy and cheerful heart.

God in His infinite kindness has showered us with His steadfast love. There was nothing we could do to earn this, or be worthy of it, yet He chose to do it anyway, He chose to be faithful to us, and to pour out His heart into us.

How can we ever show Him our thankfulness for all that He has done for us?

We can thank Him with our words, or better still we can thank Him with our lives. We can thank Him by giving ourselves to do His will, by loving His people, by the reading of His Word, by sacrificing our desires and by living a Christ-like example.

In all things, live a life worthy of the blessings that God has poured out on you, and give thanks daily for his amazing steadfast love.

In the early light of morning
I give you all my praise
I offer up thanksgiving
As my arms to you I raise.

I bless you through all circumstance
No matter what comes my way
For your goodness overwhelms me
As you walk with me through the day.

You teach me to trust in you
And depend on you alone
As you promise not to leave me
That in you I have a home.

You stay closer than a brother
And love me as your friend
You watch over me as my father
Your care for me has no end.

So from morning through to evening
I offer you all I am
And I worship you my redeemer
The almighty son of man.

Be Still

Psalm 46:10 (NIV)
'Be still and know that I am God'

This is such a beautiful verse, and it instructs us to just stop, not be distracted, or fearful, or anxious, but just take time out and rest in the knowledge of who God is.

We find it so hard to do this, we struggle with handing over all that we are doing, with letting go of all that is holding us, and just taking time out in God.

The Passion Translation says it like this 'Surrender your anxiety! Be silent and stop your striving and you will see that I am God'. This certainly gives us a deeper insight into what it is that God wants us to do. He wants us to surrender, to give up, to hand over, to stop fighting, and to be silent.

This is such a challenge for most of us, we are not used to having to be still, having nothing to worry about or fret over, we are certainly not used to the whole idea of not having to strive.

For many of us, having peace appears unobtainable, it's something we all desperately want, yet it seems so far out of our grasp. However, it would appear that our level of peace can only be as effective as our level of trust, and trust can only be truly shown in the midst of chaos, when there is nothing else to hold onto.

It is God's desire that we learn to trust Him, that we lean into Him during difficult times, that we take on His strength when we are at our weakest, and that we put our lives into His hands, knowing that He has our best interests at heart.

Today I would encourage you to practice being still. In your moments of quiet, let Him speak gently into your spirit and remind you of who He is. Take the time to get to know God intimately, so that on the hard days you are able to hand over your life and trust that He will take care of you.

It's in the whispers during the waiting
Where God's voice can find its way
To my heart that's still and listening
Keen to hear what He might say.

As I stop and rest in confidence
Knowing for me He has a plan
I lay down all I thought I knew
And reach up to take His hand.

For on this journey we take together
I know I'm not alone
He walks beside me daily
He loves me as His own.

He gives to me His breath of life
And allows me to be at peace
As He holds me through the hard times
To my soul He brings release.

So as I listen to His calling
And spend time in His embrace
I feel His loving hand upon me
My life covered by His grace.

For You Are With Me

Psalm 23:4 (NLT)

'Even when I walk through the darkest valley, I will not be afraid, for you are close beside me. Your rod and your staff protect and comfort me'

The words 'fear not' are mentioned 365 times in the bible. Once for every day of the year. God knew long before the beginning of time that we would live life afraid, full of anxious thoughts, doubts, worries, and concerns. In His kindness, He daily tells us not to fear.

When my children were little, they worried about all sorts of things. They lived secure lives, yet they were scared of the boogieman, monsters under the bed, villains and green men from outer space. It took much reassurance and convincing on our part that these things could not hurt them.

As adults we are no different to children, we too worry about things that are out of our control. Our fears could be finances, relationships, health or the future. We stew on situations and allow these things to fester in our minds until they begin to control us.

God wants us to know that He is walking close beside us, no matter what we are going through, we are not doing it alone. He is our safety and our protection, He is our bodyguard when we face the unknown, and He is our comfort when we are downtrodden.

Just as we as parents reassure our children that they are safe with us, God too does this. He assures us that He is right beside us, shoulder to shoulder, each step of the way.

If you are facing the unknown, if you are fearful of the future, of a doctor's report, or a possible retrenchment, know that God is with you, His hand is upon you, and He walks beside you each step of the way. No matter how dark your valley, God walks with you as a shining light.

My prayer is that you would trust Him and let all else fade away.

When I walk through the valley
I will choose not to fear
I will not give up or surrender
I will trust that you are near.

When darkness comes to haunt me
To steal away my peace
I will walk in your faithfulness
And trust that all anxiety will cease.

Though the shadow is all around me
I pray evil will not prevail
For you God will save me
My hope in you will never fail.

You lead me by still waters
And you cover me with grace
I'm here within your presence
And held in your embrace.

For in all things I trust you
Come what may I'll hold you tight
My Saviour, my Redeemer
In my darkness you are light.

Let God Be God

Romans 8:28 (NLT)

'And we know that for those who love God all things work together for good, for those who are called according to His purpose'

Sometimes we wonder how all things can work for good, especially when it's outside the realm of our understanding.

As human beings our minds are wired to follow particular pathways, so when life doesn't follow the order of how we think things will go, it disturbs us to our core. Yet we know God's ways are so much greater than ours. He can see the bigger picture, the beginning from the end. All we can see is the here and now, we don't know what the end result will actually look like. We may try to plan for it, but we can't possibly know what lays ahead, and a lot of times it's better that we don't.

Life isn't ours to control, and even more so, the lives of others aren't ours to control. No matter how much we think we are 'helping' the situation, or worse still, 'helping' God, what we are really doing is just getting in the way. We can make plans, of course, but we need to bring those into submission to God.

In letting go of our desire to control every situation around us, we are freeing ourselves up from anxiety, fear, turmoil, indecision, and a lack of peace. In surrendering our need to control we are allowing God to provide us with more than we could have ever hoped or dreamed, we are giving God permission to do His best for us.

When we try to be in control, we are telling God that we don't trust Him. It's showing Him that we think we can do better. Yet history has pointed out time and time again that we could never do better than God. His plans and His ways are always better than ours.

Today I encourage you to let God be God, and in doing so, know that all things will work together for good.

Although I struggle with confusion
Of how all things will go
I choose to trust you in each moment
And rest in what I know.

I know that you are goodness
And that in you there is peace
that you take all my anxiety
and give me true release.

No matter what the circumstance
It's all in your control
All I need do is surrender
And you will make me whole.

You walk with me in my day to day
And watch over me in sleep
I need not fear tomorrow
For I know my life you keep.

So as I trust in all your promises
And give to you my all
May all things work for good Lord
As I follow where you call.

Jesus is The Truth

Ephesians 6:14 (NIV)

'Stand firm then with the belt of truth buckled around your waist'

There is a great deal of difference between what is news and what is truth.

News brings us the facts and explains the situation to us, but truth comes from God and helps us to process all that we are dealing with, before He intervenes.

We can receive news of a diagnosis when we visit the doctors, but that news doesn't allow for the truth of God's healing power.

The loss of a job or career can come as unwelcome news that we weren't prepared for, but it doesn't bring with it the truth of God allowing one door to be closed so that He can open a better door for us.

Don't be fooled into thinking that everything you see or read is truth. So much of what we buy into is just another deception of the devil to shake us into fear, or worry, or desperation. He will use everything within his power to get us to take our eyes off God, the author and finisher of our faith, and onto the natural, which will bring us into anxiety and despair.

But we have the good news of Jesus. This news has been spread throughout the world, and with it the truth of who He is.

Jesus is the only truth that sets us free. We can be free from fear, doubt, illness, hurt, rejection, poverty, and lies. There is nothing that can hold us that we cannot be freed from, we need only to trust and believe in Him who is the truth.

When you are faced with news you weren't expecting, and you weren't prepared for, weigh it up against the truth of Jesus, and what His Word says. Hold onto His promises, and His declarations over you. Don't let what you see and hear define your situation, but rather, allow it to be defined by the truth of His amazing grace.

There are lies and deceptions
That come to steal your peace
That will leave you feeling broken
And fill you with disease.

It's the work of the darkness
to infiltrate your soul
to rob you of your faith in Christ
and destroy all that's whole.

But let the truth be your deliverance
As you cling to God alone
That you would know His faithfulness
And in Him would be at home.

Trust in His provisions
As you place your hope in His plan
That you would live a life of abundance
And in Him you would stand.

Let your faith be your hiding place
Your fortress and your tower
Where the truth and love of Jesus
Give you strength, hope and power.

Lay Down Your Burdens

Psalm 55:22 (ESV)

'Cast your burden on the Lord, and He will sustain you'

The word cast is the complete opposite of the word carry. The dictionary defines the word cast as 'throwing something forcefully'. This is how God wants us to handle our problems, cares and anxieties. He doesn't want us to hold onto them, but he wants us to throw them at Him, and maybe, to do so forcefully.

In the sport of angling, the fishing rod is cast out over the water. The rod is given a quick flick, and it goes across the land and into the water.

Imagine doing that with your problems, giving them either a quick flick, or a forceful throw, depending on the situation, and knowing that once they have landed at the feet of Jesus, they are no longer yours.

When something is thrown forcefully, it doesn't come back. Yet we tend to treat all our burdens like boomerangs, we might have the strength to throw them, but we keep reaching out to catch them coming back towards us. God wants us to let go, to cast our burdens on Him and then leave them there.

The fisherman, once he has cast his rod doesn't quickly reel it back in, he leaves it in place until he feels life tugging on the other end of the rod. That too is how we should be. Once the burden is cast, we leave it, not reaching out to pull it back. We stay in a place of stillness until we feel renewed life tugging at us, replacing our burden and bringing us into a place of replenishment.

I would encourage you today, whatever is weighing you down, causing you anxiety or stress, cast it on the Lord, and leave it there. Let Him take hold of whatever it is that has been holding you and allow Him to sustain you and fill you with renewed strength.

I lay before you all my burdens
My worries and my fears
I cast down all that holds me
And brings me to my knees.

I give you all the tears I cry
And those that I weep for
I hand to you all my hurts
My despair and so much more.

To you I lay bare my weaknesses
My sinfulness and pride
Search within my deepest heart
From you there's nothing that I hide.

Mould me into your image
And purify my heart
Make me a new creation
Give me a brand new start.

For today I offer unto you
My life to start anew
I ask you Lord to make me whole
And guide me with your truth.

The Refining Fire

Job 23:10 (NLT)

'But He knows where I am going. And when He tests me, I will come out as pure as gold'

It is in the fire where the refining happens. It is not in the safe or the easy, but it's in the hard times, in the valleys and in the depths of despair. It is when your security falls out from under you, when those you love walk away, when your health fades, or when you lose your job and the money starts to run out, this is when the refining takes place.

When gold is made pure and perfect, it is done so in the fire, when the heat is turned up, that is when the gold rises to the top, and everything else fades away. And so it is with us, it's in our hard times, when what we have hidden in the depths of our spirit rises to the top, allowing all else to fall away.

When Joseph was thrown into the pit, when he was sold, when he was accused of rape and ended up in prison, he continued to cry out to God. He did not give up, he did not complain and blame everything and everyone around him, he dug deep. He believed in the promises of God, he found his strength in the almighty. During his years in the refining fire, he suffered, he lost, he hurt, and yet he did not use this as an opportunity to cry out against God, he allowed himself to be melted down and then rebuilt again as pure gold.

God does not send us into the fire, but He certainly allows it to refine us into who He wants us to be. He allows the heat to build up under us, so that we are able to find out who we really are, and what we stand for.

If you find yourself in the fire today, allow it to refine you into who you will be tomorrow. Let all the lesser things in your life pass away, and let the gold come to the top, making you into that which is pure and good.

When in the fire of the furnace
Where scorching flames are all around
I stand grounded in the knowledge
That God's protection will abound.

When the enemy is at his greatest
And he turns his eyes my way
I trust only in the Saviour
Knowing His provision for each day.

I refuse to bow down to what is evil
Or to fear what lies ahead
But I hold onto His promises
And lean into God instead.

For He is with me in the fiery pit
And He models me as clay
His hand stays on me always
And leads me through each new day.

I am loved and led by Jesus
Both in the day and in the night
Therefore, I turn my back on darkness
And walk only in God's light.

A Happy Heart

Proverbs 15:13 (NIV)

'A happy heart makes the face cheerful, but heartache crushes the spirit'

Happiness is a choice.

Just as we choose other things in life, such as how to spend our day, what music to listen to, or who we will spend our time with, we also choose whether or not we are going to be happy.

Life can sometimes overwhelm us. We can be bombarded with trying times, stress, relationship issues, injustice and feelings of inadequacy. All of these things can weigh us down and leave us in a state of misery, but it's during these times that we need to continue to choose to be happy.

There are days when we need to make a conscious effort to put on a smile for those around us, to bring light into the room rather than fill it with darkness. We need to choose to be positive, rather than allow our negativity to consume us and all of those around us. How we act can have an impact on those we are in contact with and can affect their mood also.

In the moments when happiness eludes you, when there is no possible way you can have a happy heart and a cheerful face, go to God. Hand over to Him all that is going on inside you that is causing your spirit to be crushed, give Him all the hurt, the agony, and the heartache. Don't allow all that is good in your life to be blanketed over, or to be hidden away, but ask God to shine in you and through you.

Remember, that our happiness and our joy is not found in earthly treasures, but it is found in God. This gives us reason to celebrate each day, that regardless of what is going on around us, we can choose to be joyful in the Lord.

Lord fill my heart with happiness
And let your joy fill my soul
That I would bring glory to you always
And go wherever you may call.

May my face shine your goodness
So that others see your fame
Let your truth fill the whole earth
As all praise is given to your name.

On the mountain top I worship you
And offer up my praise
For your goodness overwhelms me
And in your presence I will stay.

Fill me with your joyfulness
And extend to me your grace
That I would walk in your mercy
And be held in your embrace.

For there is only you and no other
That we worship and obey
Christ the living Saviour
We bring our praise to you this day.

God Walks With Us

Isaiah 41:13 (NIV)

'For I am the Lord your God who takes hold of your right hand and says to you "Do not fear, I will help you"

To reach beautiful destinations we sometimes have to travel rocky roads. To reach the peak of a mountaintop, it's an uphill climb; and to descend to the base of a powerful waterfall, we take a downwards journey on a steep slope.

In the Israelites journey from Egypt to the promised land, they had to endure adverse conditions before they reached their abundance. They suffered through not having enough, to having just enough, until finally they had more than enough. God took them one step at a time, and in doing this He made sure they had all they needed to continue each day, but also just enough that they relied on Him.

Each of us is travelling on a different path, and we all have a different story, but we have one common thread, and that is our reliance on God. No matter what we're striving for, or pushing towards, or suffering through, our dependence and total faith in God is what upholds us and brings us to the destination that is our promised land.

We know that God holds our hand as we journey to our chosen place, we know that wherever we walk, we don't go there alone. Sometimes it can feel like we are alone, I'm sure that the Israelites felt that way, or they felt that they had been abandoned and that the desert was going to be their last resting place, yet God continued to be with them. No matter how hard the journey appears, whether it seems to be all uphill, or it's all downhill, we don't face that rocky path on our own, but God is with us.

Today as you face your mountain, know that you have no need to fear, for God goes with you, holding you and keeping you safe, and in all things He promises that He will help you; let this be your source of peace and comfort as you journey with Him.

As we travel on our journey
Our God remains the same
Yesterday, today and forever
His truth will never change.

He's the God who parts the waters
To separate the sea
And as He watched over Moses
He will watch over you and me.

When our days are filled with trouble
On all His promises we must stand
For He remains forever faithful
As He holds us in His hands.

So, as we trust always in His goodness
And remain steadfast in His Word
We have no cause to doubt Him
For all our prayers He has heard.

He's the Alpha and Omega
The beginning and the end
The one we place our hope in
Our Saviour and our friend.

Be A Mary

Luke 10:41-42 (NIV)

"Martha Martha" the Lord answered "you are worried and upset about many things, but few things are needed – or indeed only one. Mary has chosen what is better, and it will not be taken away from her"

We live in a world full of Martha's. We are women who are always doing, taking care of others, preparing and planning. Instead of being still, we find ourselves constantly busy.

In this scripture though, Jesus has described Mary, rather than Martha, as doing the 'better' thing. She sat at the feet of Jesus, and spent time in His presence, while her sister has taken on the chores around her.

During the time of having Jesus visit, the workload in the house would have been huge, and the stress levels incredibly high. The expectation of how the visit would go was of vast importance, and everything had to be perfect, after all, the Messiah was coming.

I can imagine the horror Martha would have felt, seeing her sister just sitting; not helping in the kitchen, not serving, not cleaning up, but just sitting at the feet of Jesus, taking in His every word. And if that wasn't bad enough, adding to the insult was having Jesus tell her that the choice that Mary had made was the 'better' choice.

This is the same today for all of us. We are knee deep in work, in doing, in obligation. We lose copious amounts of time doing seemingly mundane chores, yet they have to be done, and someone has to do them, and usually that someone is us. We don't make the time to just stop, sit at the feet of Jesus, and take in His every word.

I would encourage you today, to be a Mary in a world full of Martha's. Don't get so caught up in the having to do, that you lose sight of the bigger picture, which is just to be. The world won't stop if the house isn't spotless, or the grass isn't mowed, but an opportunity to spend time with Jesus may pass you by.

Don't miss this moment, do the 'better' thing today.

Lord my will is to serve you
In whatever way you call
I choose to give you my everything
And offer you my all.

May you find me in your presence
Down on bended knee
My hands raised to heaven
As I sing praises unto thee.

Let me serve where you need me
Regardless of the cost
That I would shine out your glory
To the broken and the lost.

I will give you every moment
To do with as you will
Be it busy in the kitchen
Or at your feet being still.

Let me always be a Mary
And bring honour to your name
Jesus Christ my Saviour
Yesterday, today, the same.

The Secret

Philippians 4:12-13 (TLB)

'I know how to live on almost nothing, or with everything. I have learned the secret of contentment in every situation, whether it be a full stomach or hunger, plenty or want, for I can do everything with the help of Christ who gives me the strength and power'

One of my favourite words in this passage is 'secret'.

Paul has learned the secret of being content. This speaks to us of something that is not commonly known, it's a hidden gem, and only a select group of people are in on it.

The thing about this secret of contentment though, is that it requires us to lay down all our wants, our desires, our selfishness, and to be willing to live with what we've got, and in whatever way that may look.

Paul knew what it was like to go without, he knew hunger, he knew loneliness, he knew pain. Most of us are not ready to sign up for that, we want the strength and power of Christ in our lives, but we don't really want to have to suffer for it.

Sometimes when life as we know it is stripped away, we learn to make do with what is left. When our security is no longer there, we find ourselves having to place our hope and trust elsewhere, and that elsewhere is God.

During COVID-19, the entire world found itself in a place of extreme change, life wasn't like it had always been, and the security of jobs and finances were suddenly gone, stripped away. No longer could we go out with friends and family, shopping was off the agenda, as was holidays, so what was left?

We were left with finding contentment in the small things, in the mundane, in the basics of everyday. We found that our strength came from God, and He enabled us to live a life not built on striving, but on stability. This is the true secret, that because of the strength and power of God, we can learn to be content in all circumstances, let that be your experience today.

Lord on bended knee I meet you
and raise my hands up high
I am still in your presence
As I trust you with my life.

I've learnt it's not in riches
That I'll be satisfied
But only in the hope of you
Can all else be pushed aside.

You have blessed me with all goodness
And all I am I owe to you
For in hunger, want or plenty
I've found the secret in your truth.

That You have clothed me with your power
And given me your strength
That in you I find contentment
For which I'd go to any length.

You are the God of my provision
You meet me in my need
In every situation
I am truly blessed indeed.

What Are You Thinking?

Proverbs 23:7 (ISV)
'As someone thinks within Himself, so he is'

Each thought we have is a stronghold. No matter how seemingly innocent it is, it has the power to control us and lead us into areas that God would never want us to go.

We are bombarded daily with the media and those around us telling us how we should think. They 'suggest' to us, that thinking and behaving a certain way will provide us with all that we want and need. The media portrays that if we want to be beautiful, or wanted, or desired that we are required to think only of ourselves, and to lavish all of our time and money on changing who we are.

It requires a great deal of discipline to take captive our thoughts, to not let negativity in, to not assume something about a situation, to not believe all we hear, and to not allow darkness to fester. We need to be aware of what is running through our minds, we need to stop and take stock of the choices we are making based on how we are thinking.

In order to keep our minds pure, we need to fill it with all that is good, we need to keep ourselves immersed daily in the Word of God, bringing His truth into every situation.

When we find ourselves being led astray by random thoughts that threaten our peace and lead us in the opposite direction to where God wants to take us, we need to make a conscious decision to lay down those thoughts. We need to check our spirit and test our motives, and then we need to bring those thoughts into submission to God.

Today if you find yourself in a place where your thoughts are holding you captive, hand them over to God. Ask Him to take all that is going through your mind that is not of Him, and to replace it with all that is good, that is lovely and that is pure.

Lord may my mind be ever focused
On the one who set me free
That I would stand strong in my purpose
And all you have for me.

Let me always have the mind of Christ
That my eyes would look to you
That in each and every circumstance
I would be fixed on what is true.

Fill my heart with your purity
And my thoughts with all that's right
So I'll be overcome with goodness
And live only in your light.

Show me the way of thinking
That is based on faith alone
So that I would rise above my feelings
Until your truth is my home.

I ask you to check my motives
And lead me in your way
For I want to live by your example
And in your presence I will stay.

Such A Time As This

Esther 4:14 (ICB)

'And who knows, that you might have been chosen for such a time as this'

Esther is a beautiful story of a young girl who believed in the plan and purpose of God for her life. She denied herself, and she saved her people. She allowed herself to be placed in a position that was not of her choosing but would be instrumental in changing the course of history.

Before God brought Esther into her destiny, He had been preparing her. He led her on a journey, and during that time He had given her the qualities that she would need to fulfill all that He had planned for her.

It can be that way for us, we can map out a life of our own choosing, we can make plans based on how we think our future should look, but it is God who ultimately knows what is best for us. There are so many doors that are opened and closed to us during our lifetime. When a door is closed, we are often disappointed, but we don't know what is behind that door, and maybe God has closed it for our own safety and wellbeing.

The doors that He opens for us are ones of blessing and opportunity, doors that when we step through, we come into the promised land of all that He has for us. We may find ourselves stepping through doors that are not of our choosing, but they can be the best option for us.

God has placed each of us where we are for a reason, He has a purpose and a plan in our position. Sometimes we can't see what the reason is, we may not even feel we are in the right place, but God knows the beginning from the end, He knows where we should be, and when.

Trust God in where He has placed you and believe that you have been chosen for such a time as this.

Just as God chose Esther
He too chose you and I
That we would fulfil His purpose
In bringing glory to His life.

For each of us He has a plan
A destiny to walk through
And He calls us to believe in Him
And to stand upon His truth.

Be a blessing where you're planted
And share the news of Christ
Let others see His goodness
That He would be glorified.

Stand strong and be fearless
In all that comes your way
Knowing He is with you
And walks beside you each day.

For this moment now in history
God has chosen you to rise
That you would be His messenger
And bring honour to His life.

May I Be Acceptable

Psalm 19:14 (NKJV)
'Let the words of my mouth and the meditations of my heart, be acceptable in your sight O Lord'

David knew that he was a sinner, he knew that without God intervening in his life, he was on a downward spiral towards death. He accepted that he needed God's grace, and His forgiveness, and he pleaded with the Lord to make his words and his thoughts pleasing toward Him.

Each and every one of us is a David. We are all sinners, all requiring the grace and forgiveness of God, and all hoping that the sacrifice of praise that we bring would be found acceptable.

It is much easier to offer God the words of our mouths, than the meditations of our heart. With our mouths we sing, and we offer praise, however, our hearts need to come before God blameless and pure.

The bible tells us to guard our hearts, as they are so easily deceived, so therefore, when we bring them before God, we need to remove all the dirt and deception so that we may be found acceptable.

David has been described as a 'man after God's own heart'. Yes, he was a man who failed on many occasions, he messed up, and he caused much anguish. However, his faith demonstrated that he was committed to following the Lord, and that he knew without God is his life he was nothing.

We too mess up; we fail in so many areas and without God we are alone and hopeless. It is such a great comfort to know that God loves us in the same way He loved David, that even during David's failings, He never once turned His back on him. He never left David alone to suffer, and each time that David asked God for His forgiveness, it was never withheld from Him.

This too is how God loves us. As you offer Him your words and your meditations, know that you will always be loved and acceptable in His sight.

May my words to you be pleasing
That I might bring you joy
That you would gladly hear my whisper
And the praises from my voice.

May my heart be filled goodness
That you would draw me near
That in love you would embrace me
And cast out all my fear.

Would you keep me from deception
And let my heart be purified
That to you I might surrender
To see you glorified.

I want to live a life of worship
That will honour you alone
Whether on earth or in heaven
You will be my home.

So let my words be acceptable
And my meditations bring delight
That you would shower me with your kindness
And love me with all your might.

Blood of The Lamb

Revelation 12:11 (GNT)

They won the victory over him by the blood of the Lamb and by the truth which they proclaimed; and they were willing to give up their lives and die.

We don't fight against flesh and blood, but against principalities and powers.

This is a battle we are in each day, and the way we win this is by claiming the blood that Jesus shed for us, and by our testimony of the power of God in us.

Each of us face situations in our lives that would try to dismantle us, that would endeavour to wear us down, or would cause us to become fatigued in the fight.

There are times when the battle with the enemy can be painfully hard, however, we need to always remember that the battle has not only been fought, but it has been won. When Jesus died on the cross for us, the enemy was crushed and defeated. Jesus won the victory for us, when on the cross His blood was poured out, and His final words were "It is finished ".

We can cry out Amen, as Jesus has already defeated every situation that we are facing.

We need to share the word of our testimony; we need the world to hear about the greatness of God. We need to declare His power, and to unashamedly tell of all the works of His hand. We live in a world that needs hope, it needs change, and it needs a Saviour. There are people all around us who don't know Jesus, they are fighting battles that they have no hope of winning, they need to hear from us, you and I, about the amazing life changing power of God.

Today I encourage you to claim the blood of Jesus over every situation you face, and to declare the goodness of God.

This, my friend, is how we fight the enemy and win!

I live only by the power
And the blood of the lamb
Who has fought and won the battle
For the salvation of all man.

Upon the cross that held our Saviour
Where His blood was shed for all
The veil was torn forever
As for us Christ took the fall.

He has trampled death and darkness
And opened up the door
That we might have access to the Father
And live with Him evermore.

For this I give my testimony
Of all He's done for me
From the cross to the victory
Jesus died to set me free.

I am grateful for the blood of Christ
For the death that saved my soul
That in Him I live forever
And through His sacrifice I'm made whole.

Be The Encourager

1 Thessalonians 5:11 (NIV)
'Therefore encourage one another and build each other up, just as in fact you are doing'

Each of us is called to encourage one another, to build up and not tear down. We are to cheer on our brothers and sisters, to champion them in their gifts, and to spur them on in their walk with God.

Yet so often we see the opposite of this. We see the choices of those who feel threatened by anyone and everyone, how their feelings of inadequacy or jealousy cause them to nit-pick, backstab and put others down. It would seem that any form of competition brings with it the need to fight for our place, to climb the ladder and stomp on anyone who gets in our way.

However, as Christians we know that this is not the way we should live, this is not what Jesus wants for us. His Word tells us that we are to put others first, to love like He did, and to ensure that everyone feels accepted, included and valued. He wants us to celebrate the giftings of those around us, and to support, and bless them in all that they do.

Jesus was the perfect example of this. In every aspect of His life, He went out of His way for others. It didn't matter if they were poor beggars on the street, fishermen, or tax collectors, everyone was the same in His eyes. His desire was to see them reconciled to God, healed in body, mind and spirit, and living the lives they were called to.

This too is how He wants us to live, to treat others fairly, regardless of who they are, to encourage them, and to build them up. He wants us to love in the same way He loves, not looking for fault in people, but seeing their strengths, celebrating their wins and cheering them on.

I would encourage you today to find the good in all those you meet, regardless of race, or background, or social standing, go out of your way to encourage, build up, and love, just as Jesus would do.

Lord help me to love others
With a heart that comes from you
That I would see beneath the surface
And find all that is true.

Give me eyes to see the best
And to overlook all faults
That I would see what you do
Regardless of the cost.

Help me to cheer and celebrate
When my sister has a win
Not to feel I need to beat her
But to be truly happy deep within.

Let me be an encouragement
to offer support to those in need
that they might see you Jesus
and in your strength be set free.

Lord may I follow your example
By shining light into the dark
That you would be the beacon
And the hope of every heart.

On Wings of Eagles

Isaiah 40:31 (MSG)
'But those who wait upon God get fresh strength. They spread their wings and soar like eagles, they run and don't get tired, they walk and don't lag behind'

There is such hope in this scripture. The hope for the tired, the worn out, the emotionally frazzled, and the mentally drained.

God's Word tells us that those who wait on Him, those who trust in Him, will be given fresh strength. That they would mount up on wings like eagles.

These incredible birds of prey are strong, they have muscular legs, large beaks and formidable talons. Eagles are known to be brave and courageous; they have a forceful determination. They can see their prey from a long way off, and they are single minded in the attack. The wings of an eagle can spread to over two metres, and as they fly through the air, they are beautifully graceful.

This is what we are promised, that as we trust in God, we would have renewed strength that would enable us to fly on wings like eagles.

This is such a beautiful picture for us to hold onto, all the amazing attributes of the eagle, especially their power, their courage, and their determination, is something that is available to each of us.

God our creator, our giver of life, wants us to fly, to run, and to be full of strength. He wants to renew us, to revive us and bring us into a place of soaring through the sky. All we need to do is to wait on Him, to place our trust fully in Him. He doesn't want us to battle on our own, to keep striving, to keep working, and wearing ourselves out. God in His goodness wants to give us all that He can to make our lives richer, He is fully invested in making each of us the best that we can be.

I would encourage you today to draw near to God, and to allow Him to renew your strength and set you free to soar on the wings of an eagle.

Lord I wait patiently in your presence
That you might give me strength
That you would lift me in my time of need
And speak to me at length.

I pray for wings like an eagle
That would soar through the sky
With power and with courage
Set free that I might fly.

Fill my lungs with breath from you
And enable me to run
Free me from my weariness
And from all that leaves me undone.

I want to lay my life before you
And trust you in all my ways
So let me not grow faint Lord
But to walk with you each day.

In the morning and the evening
I give all I am to you
As I wait for your renewal
I know that you will see me through.

www.ingramcontent.com/pod-product-compliance
Lightning Source LLC
Chambersburg PA
CBHW071426090426
42737CB00011B/1585

* 9 7 8 0 6 4 5 2 2 7 7 0 3 *